**SHAMBHALA
CLASSICS**

To dearest Betty Jo,
in gratitude for the
Path you have chosen.
Yours in love, as we
both release into the
Mystery, Jerry
Christmas 2004

Shāntideva

THE WAY
OF THE
BODHISATTVA

A TRANSLATION OF THE
Bodhicharyāvatāra

TRANSLATED FROM THE TIBETAN
BY THE PADMAKARA TRANSLATION GROUP

FOREWORD BY THE DALAI LAMA

SHAMBHALA
Boston & London
2003

SHAMBHALA PUBLICATIONS, INC.
HORTICULTURAL HALL
300 MASSACHUSETTS AVENUE
BOSTON, MASSACHUSETTS 02115
www.shambhala.com

© 1997 by the Padmakara Translation Group

9 8 7 6 5 4 3 2 1

Printed in the United States of America

⊗ This edition is printed on acid-free paper that meets
the American National Standards Institute z39.48 Standard.

Distributed in the United States by Random House, Inc.,
and in Canada by Random House of Canada Ltd

Library of Congress Cataloging-in-Publication Data
Śāntideva, 7th cent.
[Bodhicaryāvatāra. English]
The way of the Bodhisattva: a translation of the
Bodhicaryāvatāra / Shāntideva.
p.   cm.—(Shambhala dragon editions)
Translated from Tibetan.
ISBN 1-57062-253-1 (alk. paper)
ISBN 1-59030-057-2 (Shambhala Classics)
1. Mahayana Buddhism—Doctrines—Early works to 1800.
I. Series.
BQ3142.E5   1997   96-25650
294.3'85—DC20   CIP

CONTENTS

FOREWORD

The *Bodhicharyavatara* was composed by the Indian scholar Shantideva, renowned in Tibet as one of the most reliable of teachers. Since it mainly focuses on the cultivation and enhancement of Bodhichitta, the work belongs to the Mahayana. At the same time, Shantideva's philosophical stance as expounded particularly in the ninth chapter on wisdom, follows the Prasangika Madhyamika viewpoint of Chandrakirti.

The principal focus of Mahayana teachings is on cultivating a mind wishing to benefit other sentient beings. With an increase in our own sense of peace and happiness we will naturally be better able to contribute to the peace and happiness of others. Transforming the mind and cultivating a positive, altruistic and responsible attitude is beneficial right now. Whatever problems and difficulties we may have, we can thereby face them with courage, calmness and high spirits. Therefore, it is also the very root of happiness for many lives to come.

Based on my own little experience I can confidently say that the teachings and instructions of the Buddhadharma and particularly the Mahayana teachings continue to be relevant and useful today. If we sincerely put the gist of these teachings into practice, we need have no hesitation about their effectiveness. The benefits of developing qualities like love, compassion, generosity, and patience are not confined to the personal level alone; they extend to all sentient beings and even to the maintenance of harmony with the environment. It is not as if these teachings were useful at some time in the past but are no longer relevant in modern times. They remain pertinent today. This is why I encourage people to pay attention to such practices; it is not just so that the tradition may be preserved.

The *Bodhicharyavatara* has been widely acclaimed and respected for more than one thousand years. It is studied and praised by all four schools of Tibetan Buddhism. I myself received transmission and explanation of this important, holy text from the late Kunu Lama, Tenzin Gyaltsen, who received it from a disciple of the great Dzogchen master, Dza Patrul Rinpoche. It has proved very useful and beneficial to my mind.

I am delighted that the Padmakara Translation Group has prepared a fresh English translation of the *Bodhicharyavatara*. They have tried to combine an accuracy of meaning with an ease of expression, which can only serve the text's purpose well. I congratulate them and offer my prayers that their efforts may contribute to greater peace and happiness among all sentient beings.

TENZIN GYATSO
THE FOURTEENTH DALAI LAMA
17 October 1996

INTRODUCTION

The Way of the Bodhisattva[1] is one of the great classics of the Mahāyāna, the Buddhism of the Great Vehicle. Presented in the form of a personal meditation, but offered in friendship to whoever might be interested, it is an exposition of the path of the bodhisattvas—those beings who, turning aside from the futility and sufferings of saṃsāra, nevertheless renounce the peace of an individual salvation and vow to work for the deliverance of all beings and to attain the supreme enlightenment of buddhahood for their sake. As such, Shāntideva's work embodies a definition of compassion raised to its highest power and minutely lays out the methods by which this is to be achieved. It is an overwhelming demonstration of how concern for others, in a love that wholly transcends desire and concern for self, lies at the core of all true spiritual endeavor and is the very heart of enlightened wisdom.

The author of *The Way of the Bodhisattva* was a member of the monastic university of Nālandā, which, like the other great university of Vikramashila, was one of the most celebrated centers of learning in ancient India. Little is known about him, although a number of colorful legends have come down to us over the centuries—tantalizing half-lights that give us a glimpse of a highly unusual and independent personality. It would seem that Shāntideva was very much his own master, temperamentally impervious to social and ecclesiastical pressures, and able to pursue his insights irrespective of conventional expectations and public opinion.[2] He was drawn at an early age to the wisdom teachings of the Mahāyāna, as embodied in the bodhisattva Mañjushrī, and thus to the Mādhyamika or Centrist school of Buddhist philosophy, renowned for its profundity and dialectic subtlety. Yet, as his work reveals, Shāntideva was by no means a dry academic. Like Nāgārjuna before him, he possessed to a remarkable degree the unusual combination of a powerful intelligence linked with a keen appreciation of the sufferings of the world and a deep sense of tenderness toward others.

It is impossible here to give an adequate description of Shāntideva's great poem, but it is hoped that with the passage of time it will be possible to make available translations of the commentaries by the great masters of the past. The following introduction is intended only as a guideline to help readers find their bearings, especially those who are unfamiliar with fundamental Buddhist ideas.

It is a frequent practice among commentators to divide *The Way of the Bodhisattva* into three main sections, along the lines of a famous prayer attributed to Nāgārjuna:

> May bodhichitta, precious and sublime,
> Arise where it has not yet come to be;
> And where it has arisen may it never fail
> But grow and flourish ever more and more.

According to this scheme, the first three chapters ("The Excellence of Bodhichitta," "Confession," and "Commitment") are designed to stimulate the dawning of bodhichitta in the mind. The following three chapters ("Awareness," "Vigilance," and "Patience") give instructions on how to prevent the precious attitude from being dissipated, while the seventh, eighth, and ninth chapters ("Heroic Perseverance," "Meditation," and "Wisdom") prescribe ways in which bodhichitta may be progressively intensified. The tenth chapter is a concluding prayer of dedication.

THE DAWN OF BODHICHITTA

What is bodhichitta? The word has many nuances and is easier to understand, perhaps, than to translate. For this reason we have used the Sanskrit term, in the hope that by dint of careful definition it may be incorporated into and allowed to enrich our language. *Chitta* means "mind," "thought," "attitude." *Bodhi* means "enlightenment," "awakening," and is cognate with the term *buddha* itself. This gives us "mind of enlightenment," "awakening mind"—the attitude of mind that tends toward, and is imbued with, enlightenment, the specific characteristic of buddhahood. It should be noted that *bodhichitta* is not a synonym for *compassion*; it is a broader term in which compassion is implied.

According to tradition, bodhichitta is said to have two aspects, or rather to exist on two levels. First, one speaks of absolute bodhichitta, referring to the direct cognizance of reality. This is the wisdom of emptiness: an immediate, nondual insight that transcends conceptualization. Second, there is relative bodhichitta, by which is meant the aspiration to attain the highest good, or buddhahood, for the sake of all, together with all the practical steps necessary to achieve this goal. The connection between these two bodhichittas—the wisdom of emptiness on the one hand, the will to deliver beings from suffering on the other—is not perhaps immediately clear. But within the Buddhist perspective, as Shāntideva gradually reveals, absolute and relative bodhichitta are two interdependent aspects of the same thing. The true realization of emptiness is impossible without the practice of perfect compassion, while no compassion can ever be perfect without the realization of the wisdom of emptiness.

At first sight, this suggests an impasse in which bodhichitta is logically impossible to realize, for how could one ever penetrate the closed circle? It is nevertheless the startling assertion of Buddhist teaching that the mind itself, even the mind in saṃsāra, is never, and never has been, ultimately alienated from the state of enlightenment. Bodhichitta is in fact its true nature and condition. The mind is not identical with the defilement and distraction that beset and sometimes overwhelm it, and thus it may be freed from them; it is capable of growth and improvement and may be trained. By using methods and tools grounded in the duality of subject and object, the mind has the power to evolve toward a wisdom and a mode of being (in fact its own true nature) that utterly transcends this duality. At present, of course, for most of us, this is something that remains to be seen, something to take on trust. And so it is with an extraordinary didactic skill, and with an immediacy and relevance that the lapse of a thousand years has done nothing to diminish, that Shānti-deva brings to our attention the realities of egocentric existence, in all its pain and idiocy, and places before us the vision of a wholly new alternative, together with a practical instruction whereby that vision may become an actual experience.

For all its practicability, however, the fact remains that the first stirrings of bodhichitta in the mind are profoundly mysterious, for what could possibly be their origin? "This state of mind so precious and so rare arises truly wondrous, never seen before." Indeed, given the habitual orientation of the mind, fixed as it is upon the supposed reality of ego and phenomena, rooted in the duality of subject and object, wandering in samsāra from beginningless time—that an impulse toward perfect altruism and self-forgetting can arise at all seems nothing short of miraculous. What could go more radically against the grain? To say that it is possible is an impressive affirmation of the mind's potential. Even so, bodhichitta is itself so extraordinary that its first impulses appear to come from outside.

> As when a flash of lightning rends the night,
> And in its glare shows all the dark black clouds had hid,
> Likewise rarely, through the buddhas' power,
> Virtuous thoughts rise, brief and transient, in the world. (1.5)

It is in this same spirit of an external prompting that Shāntideva begins his poem. The first chapter consists of a rhapsodic celebration of bodhichitta intended to fill the mind with enthusiasm and orientate it toward a new and wonderful goal. Shāntideva encourages himself and his fortunate readers, first toward an interest, then toward practical engagement, in the bodhisattva path.

Shāntideva's pedagogical method, pursued throughout the poem and already familiar from the teachings of the Buddha himself, is simple and effective: first encouragement through reflection on the advantages and excellence of the objective, then a stimulus through meditation on the dire consequences of weakness and recidivism. His basic rule of thumb is that ground gained must be retained at all cost and never yielded. Once attention has been caught, and interest kindled, the task is one of consolidation: the original impulse and fervor must be safe-guarded and never allowed to disappear. The importance of this is only too obvious. One has only to consider the sheer fragility of normal, everyday mental states. "Virtuous thoughts rise, brief and transient . . . ," and it is one of the most alarming aspects of spiritual and moral life that insights, left unattended and without support, will invariably fade. Realizations evaporate and enthusiasm drains away into the sands of inadvertence and old habits. It is possible to embark on the practice of Dharma with great energy and interest but later, perhaps years later, to turn away empty-handed, with nothing to show for all the time taken.

Thus, for Shāntideva, as with the Buddhist tradition in general, in the education of the mind—one's own mind—fear and the dread of the consequences of evil are tools as legitimate as those of enthusiasm and encouragement. It is in this spirit of mental training that Shāntideva places before us the unpalatable facts of human existence: its fragility, its impermanence, the certainty and horrible realities of death, and the possibility, if not probability, of postmortem suffering in infernal torment. Perhaps it is because the stakes are so high that he tears away so mercilessly the pretenses and facile optimism with which we veil the facts, trying to convince ourselves that "after all, things are not so bad." To those new to Buddhadharma, it often comes as a surprise that in a tradition that places such a high premium on love and compassion, so much attention should be given to the sufferings of the lower states: those of animals, of famished ghosts, and the hell realms. The scriptures and commentaries abound in detailed descriptions, and Buddhist iconography can be horrifyingly explicit. To the unprepared Westerner, the shock is often severe. And no doubt through an overhasty comparison with similar themes (rightly or wrongly understood), as these have played themselves out in the history of European and Near Eastern religious thought, the Buddhist ideas are not infrequently dismissed as being of morbid and sadistic origin.

Superficial similarity, however, masks a radical difference. According to Buddhist teaching, the definition of moral good or evil is made exclusively in terms of cause and effect. An act is considered evil, negative, nonvirtuous, or sinful, not because it is a transgression of a divinely ordained principle laid down by the creator of the universe, but because it is productive of suffering in this or future existences. Virtue, on the other hand, is that which brings about happiness and tends to spiritual development. The experiences of the infernal states are the ineluctable result of evil attitudes and actions. Whether or not the modern Westerner wishes to believe in the real existence of infernal realms is in a sense beside the point. Evil simply brings forth suffering; and it hardly matters whether one conceives of this in the picturesque terms of Dante's inferno or shares the view of Jean-Paul Sartre that "hell is other people." Nevertheless, it is important to grasp that the idea of an *eternal* damnation as a *punishment* for sin is foreign to Buddhist understanding. Suffering is a consequence of one's own action, not a retribution inflicted by an external power. Infernal torments, moreover, though they may last for aeons, belong to saṃsāra and are therefore not exempt from the law of impermanence. And even if the notion of a divine vengeance is regarded as an approximation, in mythological terms, to the concept of karmic consequences, it is perhaps worth suggesting that the impersonal view proposed by Buddhism should have the advantage of exorcising the paralyzing sense of guilt, or revolt, that can so often be the outcome of a too anthropomorphic theism. The doctrine of karma has only one message: the experience of states of being follows upon the perpetration of acts. We are the authors of our own destiny; and being the authors, we are ultimately, perhaps frighteningly, free.

With regard to *The Way of the Bodhisattva,* there are two things we should notice. The first is that not only does Shāntideva accept the reality of the lower realms, he literally forces them on our attention. This has the educative purpose mentioned above, but it also reveals a vital characteristic of the bodhisattva's attitude. Shāntideva's constant and overwhelming concern is with the predicament of his fellow beings, and from their pain and degradation he does not avert his eyes. He is ready to confront suffering in all its horrifying reality, and having abandoned all thought for his own comfort and security, he does not draw back in fear or revulsion. He gazes into the heart of darkness unflinchingly, with an intense fixity of purpose. He is prepared to accompany the damned into the pit. He is neither revolted nor depressed, being one who in compassion "will venture in the hell of unremitting agony, as swans sweep down upon a lotus lake" (8.107). The keynote is courage, and time and time again in *The Way of the Bodhisattva*, compassion emerges not as a sorrowing, lachrymose state of mind, but as a protective concern that is vibrant with joy and heroic confidence.

The second thing to note is that in Shāntideva's description of sufferings, there is a notable absence of moral comment or judgment. This is brought out clearly in the tenth chapter where the merits of composition are dedicated to the emptying of the hells and the deliverance of the damned. The fires are quenched in a rain of flower-scented water, the glaciers are thawed, the damned are set free and comforted by the presence of the great bodhisattvas. It is a wonderful vision, and we are borne along by its beauty. But where, we might ask, is the justice in it? Shāntideva's obvious wish is simply to save from suffering, with no questions asked. We on the other hand might protest, with a sense of moral indignation and in the name of right, that the damned are where they are for good reason. They are, after all, the serial killers, the child murderers, the tyrants of evil regimes, the perpetrators of pogroms, the ethnic cleansers and the keepers of the death camps, the witch hunters, the interrogators, the torturers, the inquisitors.

The sheer strength and impartiality of Shāntideva's compassion seem to be a subversion of universal order. In a sense they are, for they point to a new vision of things ultimately grounded not in the concepts of right and wrong, but in compassion and the wisdom of emptiness. Instead of dividing the universe now and forever into twin compartments of good and evil, the sinners and the just, the blessed and the damned, Buddhism focuses on the predicament of saṃsāra as such.

In saṃsāra, as we have noted, all experiences, of pleasure and of pain, have their roots in previous action. The mind, conditioned by ignorance, attraction, and aversion, can only respond egocentrically to situations as they arise, contriving its own evolution, favorable or otherwise as the case may be. It passes through a stream of temporary experiences that are all fundamentally flawed by suffering or the possibility of suffering—experiences that lead nowhere and which are thus always and necessarily meaningless. It would, however, be a ridiculous mistake to accuse Shāntideva of moral nihilism, or to suppose that he is in revolt against the doctrine of karma. Yet his unconditional compassion draws out attention to the fact that the law of karma does not amount to a theory of human justice, neither does it provide the basis for feelings of moral outrage or ethical superiority. In any case, since experience is the fruit of action, it must follow that in saṃsāra—and this in certain contexts may be difficult to accept—there can be no ultimately innocent victims. In response to this, Buddhism teaches that the object of compassion is simply suffering itself. It would, after all, be absurd to withdraw compassion from the "guilty" and reserve it only for the "worthy," those assumed to be morally innocent—for the simple reason that in saṃsāra, there are no worthy objects in this sense. For Shāntideva on the other hand, since suffering is all-pervasive, all beings, at all times and regardless of circumstances, are worthy objects. Relatively speaking, of course, the concepts of right and wrong are crucial, and for the practitioner, the importance of pure ethics is fundamental. But to cling to moral values in a spirit of self-righteousness and as a means of judging others is evidence of superficiality and ego-clinging and does not form part of the bodhisattva's mental horizon.

In any case, the vow of the bodhisattva is to deliver beings from suffering, in other words to deliver them from the causes of their suffering. The work of the buddha or bodhisattva is therefore to teach, to show the way—first by revealing values to be adopted or abandoned (and thus the means whereby wholesome and propitious existential states are produced), then by teaching the wisdom whereby saṃsāra is wholly transcended. This is of course the definition of Dharma; the *Bodhicharyāvatāra* is itself Shāntideva's liberating message to the world.

Despite the occasional somberness of the picture, Shāntideva's teaching is profoundly optimistic. If suffering is the fruit of thought and action, it can be avoided. The realization that we are in a position to change ourselves and so shape our destiny, leads logically to confession, the subject of Shāntideva's second chapter. Here it should be understood that although regret is naturally entailed, this does not involve an orgy of guilty breast-beating or exaggerated feelings of inadequacy. In Buddhism, confession is to be understood principally in the sense of open acknowledgment—primarily to oneself—of past behavior. When former actions and one's own nature are confronted, when old behavior patterns and tendencies are raised into consciousness, then and only then can they be changed; then and only then is a new direction possible. It is interesting to note that, having called upon the buddhas and bodhisattvas and declared his guilt, Shāntideva does not ask them for forgiveness. They are invoked as protectors and the supreme witnesses of his self-disclosure and resolve. It is in their presence that an old course comes to an end and a new one begins.

And so, borne along on a wave of elation and confidence, supported by the glorious vision of the attainments of the buddhas and great beings of the past, and spurred by the realization that time is short and the stakes high, Shāntideva is impelled (in chapter 3) toward commitment to the bodhisattva path—in words that have since become the standard formula, in the Tibetan tradition, for the taking of the bodhisattva vow.[3]

❁ PROTECTING AND MAINTAINING BODHICHITTA

That the original resolve of bodhichitta needs consolidation becomes evident from the very first stanzas of chapter 4, where Shāntideva takes stock of what he has just done and begins to count the cost. The undertaking to which he has committed himself in a moment of optimistic zeal is devastating. Hesitation is understandable. However, in view of the alternatives, and in order to stiffen his resolve, Shāntideva embarks on a graphic description of the dreadful consequences of retraction. As always, the aim is pedagogical. Shāntideva is no tub-thumping preacher content merely to terrorize his listeners. The situation as he describes it is certainly grim, but he shows the way out and in so doing plots out a scheme of mental training that, for its spiritual profundity and psychological acuity, has rarely been equaled and surely never surpassed anywhere or at any time in the history of the world's religions.

The first message is that, however immense the goal may seem, it *is* possible—provided that we want it and make the necessary effort. We can *learn* to be free and to become buddhas. Moreover, Shāntideva points out that having attained a human existence, we are at a crossroads; we have reached a critical point. According to Buddhism, human life, at once so precious and so fragile, is the existential opportunity par excellence. Of all forms of existence, it is the only one in which development along a spiritual trajectory is truly possible. And yet the occasion is easily, in fact habitually, squandered in trivial pursuits. Time passes, and we "measure out our lives in coffee spoons." Perceiving the nature of the opportunity, and realizing how it is slipping through his fingers, Shāntideva responds with almost a note of panic:

> For it's as if by chance that I have gained
> This state so hard to find, wherein to help myself.
> And now, when freedom—power of choice—is mine,
> If once again I'm led away to hell,
>
> I am as if benumbed by sorcery,
> My mind reduced to total impotence
> With no perception of the madness overwhelming me.
> O what is it that has me in its grip? (4.26–27)

The situation is certainly perilous, but what is it that constitutes the danger? It is the *kleshas*, defiled emotions: "Anger, lust—these enemies of mine." These are the roots of sorrow, to which every suffering, be it on a personal or cosmic scale, can ultimately be traced. And yet these kleshas, however terrible they may be in their effects, are nothing more than thoughts: intangible, fleeting mental states. To become aware of this fact, and to see therefore that our destiny lies in the way we are able to order the workings of our minds, is the theme of the fourth chapter. How is it, Shāntideva asks, that mere thoughts can cause so much havoc? The answer is simply that we allow them to do so. "I it is who welcome them within my heart." With these words, the battle lines are drawn. The enemy is the afflictions, the thoughts of pride, anger, lust, jealousy, and the rest. The arena is the mind itself. Shāntideva steels himself for the fray, giving himself confidence by stimulating his own sense of pride and self-worth. As a method, this is highly original and very characteristic of Shāntideva's pragmatic approach—a sort of psychological homeopathy, in which an attitude normally considered a defilement is consciously and strenuously adopted as an antidote to defilement itself. The theme is developed at greater length later on in the book, but for the time being, chapter 4 concludes on a ringing note of aggression. Emotional defilements are the enemy; they must be destroyed. "This shall be my all-consuming passion; filled with rancor I will wage my war!" Paradoxically, the conflict need not be an arduous one. Thoughts after all are merely thoughts. Through analysis and skill, they can be easily eliminated. Once scattered by the eye of wisdom and driven from the mind, they are by definition totally destroyed. And yet Shāntideva reflects, with sentiments that must go to the heart of every would-be disciple: "But oh—my mind is feeble. I am indolent!"

Once it is clear, however, that the problem lies in the mind itself, or rather in the emotions that arise there, the simple but difficult task is to become aware of how thoughts emerge and develop. This is the theme of the fifth chapter, on vigilance. Again we find the same note of practical optimism. Just as the mind is the source of every suffering, likewise it is the wellspring of every joy. And once again, the good news is that the mind can be controlled and trained.

If, with mindfulness' rope,
The elephant of the mind is tethered all around,
Our fears will come to nothing,
Every virtue drop into our hands. (5.3)

The essential problem, which a moment's reflection on experience will confirm, is not that defilements occur within our minds, but that nine times out of ten, we are not aware that they are there. Or rather, that by the time they obtrude upon our waking consciousness, they have usually acquired such dimensions and strength that in the ordinary run of things we are powerless to prevent their consequences. The sudden outburst of destructive anger, the lustful impulse, the cruel or arrogant word that can have life-changing consequences, must have had their source, perhaps a long time previously, in a momentary flash of impatience or desire that, had it been adverted to at the time, might easily have been neutralized and dispelled. All very well, but how precisely is one to become so perfectly self-possessed that no impulse of the mind, however slight, is able to pass unnoticed? Alas, there are no magical solutions. The technique prescribed by Shāntideva is that of constant, unrelenting vigilance—a continuous advertence to what is happening within the inner forum. He says that we should guard our minds with the same care with which we would protect a broken or wounded arm while moving through an unruly crowd; and here again, the educative methods of fear and encouragement have their place. Shāntideva recommends that as soon as we feel the urge to do anything—to speak or even to walk across the room—we should get into the habit of self-scrutiny. The slightest impulses to negativity should be greeted with a total paralysis of the system: "It's then that like a log you should remain." No thought should be allowed to develop into action unchallenged. Given the required degree of self-awareness, it comes as no surprise that Shāntideva should refer to the minutiae of everyday behavior—all the little things we habitually overlook, excusing ourselves with the thought that they are too insignificant to bother about. In such a practice, in fact, it is precisely the small, practically subliminal impulses and behavior patterns that require the closest attention. And in any case, everything we do affects the world. Any action can be the cause, or the cause of the cause, of another's suffering. Thus the way we eat, walk, move furniture around, even matters of personal hygiene—all are significant.

A heightening of consciousness of the kind Shāntideva advocates is liable to awaken an understanding of something that for most of us passes, if not actually unnoticed, at least unexamined. This is the peculiar infatuation that the mind has with its physical support. We love our bodies and are deeply involved in them. We are engrossed in their sensations to the point that we identify them as ourselves and invent philosophies, and theologies, to justify this. Like the Buddha before him, Shāntideva calls all this into question, pointing out how strange it is that the mind should identify with, and find desirable, something so external to itself, so fragile, so ultimately disappointing and, in its constituent parts, so repulsive as the physical body. In relation to its own bodily support and that of other beings, the mind seems to move in a dimension that is almost entirely one of make believe; and it is an extraordinary paradox that it can experience the most powerful yearning for something by which, on closer inspection, it is almost invariably repelled. Nevertheless, Shāntideva does not in any way repudiate the body, and the spirit of destructive asceticism and repression is as foreign to him as to any other Buddhist teacher. The body has its place and value, but the mind must be freed from an obsessive and enslaving preoccupation with it.

Reflections on the status of the body and the importance played by it in the context of personal experience are developed at length in the chapter on patience. Coming at the conclusion of the section devoted to the protection of bodhichitta, patience is celebrated as the supreme austerity. It is the antidote to anger, regarded in Buddhism as the most destructive and perilous of all mental factors. Anger, defined as the flooding of the mind with violent and aggressive feelings, leading naturally to hostility and conflict, is outlawed in Buddhism as in no other religious tradition. Even so-called righteous anger, so often excused as having injustice and abuse as its object, is utterly condemned if this involves the overpowering of the mind in a wave of uncontrollable and destructive passion. Aside from a purely external and as it were artificial indignation, put on for educational purposes—which has compassion as its motive and is acted out by one whose mind is under control—anger has absolutely no place in the scheme of spiritual development. It is totally inimical to mental training and will ruin and annihilate in an instant all progress and merit gained.

This being so, the crucial question of how to behave in a hostile environment begins to emerge. Step by step, Shāntideva focuses on the real source of the problem, the basis of anger as of every other defilement. This is the ego, the self, the sense of "I," experienced as the center of the universe, a universe interpreted as friend or enemy in relation to how it is perceived from the egocentric viewpoint. In Buddhism, this is of course the central issue, and it is only in the light of the full teachings on emptiness that it can be satisfactorily discussed. For the moment, however, Shāntideva remains on the level of relative practice. His concern is to show how the problem of enemies—aggression and retaliation—can be dealt with in the context of everyday experience. His arguments are ingenious, his logic relentless; and by the end of the chapter one is forced to see not only that anger must never be allowed to develop, but that situations of conflict, endured and resolved through patience, are invaluable, in fact indispensable, as occasions for spiritual growth. Patience, as Shāntideva describes it, implies an almost incredible degree of resilience and courage, the courage of a Mahatma Gandhi or a

Martin Luther King. Far from being a sort of limp and spineless acquiescence, as Nietzsche would have us believe, Shāntideva's patience is the ultimate heroism, fearlessness perfected to the highest intensity.

Shāntideva points out that anger, the normal reaction to hostility and adversity, achieves nothing but to increase our sufferings. It is our "sorrow-bearing enemy." As such it is to be eliminated; and in a way that we have by now come to expect, Shāntideva rises to the challenge, heartening himself with cheerful words. In any case, suffering, though of course unwanted, has its uses. Without it we would be like the gods, never longing for release from saṃsāra. It humbles our pride and engenders sympathy toward those who also suffer. Even virtue comes to seem attractive!

Irritation arises naturally in the mind against fellow creatures perceived as unpleasant or threatening, and it seems normal to resent the aggressor. But Shāntideva asks us to be less superficial. When we suffer the physical discomforts of illness, for example, we know very well that the pain is due to bodily imbalances. We may dislike the pain, but it would be absurd to resent it angrily. In the same way, the hostile behavior of an enemy does not arise spontaneously; it too is the product of causes and conditions. Why resent someone who is himself the victim of emotional defilement? The very act of identifying the aggressor as a really existing ego over against our own (instead of being aware simply of an interplay of impersonal psychophysical forces) is itself unjustified. That which strikes us as the unruly behavior of other beings may indeed be difficult to put up with; but when we understand the reality of the situation, the inconvenience becomes easier to manage. Thus when we are attacked, it is important to remember that the aggressor, acting on the impulse of his own defilements, is creating the causes of his own suffering. Knowing this, Shāntideva says, "Even if compassion does not rise in us, we can at least refrain from being angry." In any case, viewed objectively, enemies can only be of two kinds. Either they are intrinsically hostile, in which case to resent their behavior is as absurd as to resent fire for being hot; or they are fundamentally well disposed but have momentarily succumbed to a crisis of defilement. Here, too, animosity is out of place: it is as foolish as resenting the sky for being covered with clouds. Besides, when someone hits me with a stick, I am angry not with the stick but with the one who holds it. By the same token it is illogical to hate my enemy. He may wield the stick, but he is himself in the grip of his defilements. It is the emotion of which he is the victim that I should resent.

Taking his argument a step further, Shāntideva points out that in any conflict, the victim and aggressor are both caught up in a situation of mutual dependence. In the case of a physical attack, for example, if pain occurs, it has two equally important sources corresponding to the two terms of the experience. The fact that suffering happens depends as much on the degree to which the victim's mind clings to his body as on the wound inflicted by the aggressor.

> Their weapons and my body—
> Both are causes of my suffering!
> They their weapons drew, while I held out my body.
> Who then is more worthy of my anger? (6.43)

Once again, all experience is karmically conditioned. Events that seem beyond our control are in fact the fruits of former actions, which means that it is incorrect to claim that the enemy is nothing but an aggressor. "Those who harm me come against me, summoned by my evil karma." Even more, given the consequences of the enemies' evil deeds, and also the great results of patience in the face of adversity, we arrive at the paradoxical conclusion: "Therefore I am their tormentor! Therefore it is they who bring me benefit." And with these words, Shāntideva reduces to absurdity the conventional approach to the hostility of aggressors.

Pursuing the argument yet further, Shāntideva shows how the enemy is not merely the object of tolerance; he is to be cherished as an indispensable helper on the bodhisattva path. Our enemy does for us what no friend or loved one can do. By awakening us to the reality of our own ego-clinging, the enemy provides opportunities for patience, purification, the exhaustion of evil karma. And so the inevitable conclusion:

They, like Buddha's very blessing,
Bar my way, determined as I am
To plunge myself headlong in sorrow—
How could I be angry with them? (6.101)

❀ INTENSIFYING BODHICHITTA

Shāntideva now moves on to the culminating chapters of his great work and sets out ways in which bodhichitta may be intensified to the highest pitch. As in chapters 1 and 4, he begins by whipping up a sense of urgency and enthusiasm. Here the stark realities of the proximity of death and the possibility of rebirth in the infernal states are forced upon us with unprecedented force. If we squander the incredible opportunity for liberation afforded by this human existence, how will we feel when the servants of the Lord of Death make their appearance and the din of hell breaks upon our ears? Moreover, however well off and virtuous we may think we are at the present time, Shāntideva assures us that, lodged in our mind streams, from time without beginning, we have karmic residues more than sufficient to precipitate a disastrous fall.

The hells in which the boiling molten bronze
Will burn your body, tender like a baby's flesh—
All is now prepared, your former deeds have done it!
How can you lie back, so free of care? (7.12)

This human life indeed is not the time for complacency. And yet, as always, Shāntideva's message is full of hope and practical assurance. We have this opportunity now; our destiny is in our own hands. "Take advantage," he says "of this human boat, free yourself from sorrow's mighty stream." The requisite qualities are courage and a steadfast refusal to give up. Shāntideva points out that to let ourselves off the hook with the excuse that the effort is beyond us, far from corresponding with the facts, is nothing but indolence and cowardice. After all, with perseverance, even insects have it in them to gain liberation. Here again we find the theme of pride as a positive tool in the task of maintaining one's resolve. Shāntideva develops this at great length, distinguishing wholesome confidence from arrogance, in a kind of word play (hardly possible to bring out in translation) that results in a sort of humorous riddle. As before, and despite more somber reflections, the general tone is overwhelmingly positive. To shelter themselves from the midday sun, elephants will plunge into the waters of a lake. Just so, bodhisattvas throw themselves into their great work for beings. Chapter 7 concludes on a note of calm, immovable resolve.

The bodhisattva in training, with an intention consolidated by awareness, vigilance, and the perfection of patience, and stirred by the desire to labor unrelentingly until the goal is reached, now proceeds to embrace the real, the truly mind-transforming discipline. The eighth chapter, on meditation, which is the culmination of the teachings on the level of relative bodhichitta, falls into two main sections. First there is a preliminary instruction on how to create the proper environment for the meditation (the first ninety stanzas). Then there follows a lengthy description of the meditation itself. Shāntideva presents the case from the standpoint of monastic renunciation. He was himself a monk and it will be remembered that the first public reading of the *Bodhicharyāva-tāra* was given to the monastic assembly at Nālandā. Even so, it would be a mistake for the lay practitioner to dismiss Shāntideva's teaching as being exclusively relevant to ordained clerics. On the contrary, Shānti-deva delineates principles of universal validity that are in fact mandatory for everyone wishing to follow a path of profound and effective spiritual transformation.

The chapter begins, as we might expect, with a demand for concentration and the elimination of mental wandering. And the point is driven home that, whether one enters a monastery or prefers to remain in the lay condition, there can be no progress in concentration without a severe reduction in one's involvement in worldly affairs. Naturally, the external observances of the monastic rule is understood to be peculiarly propitious to the development of mental calm, but in the last analysis, it is inner motive and personal discipline that count. Thus we are counseled at length to be careful about the company we keep, recognizing the simple fact that an unexamined lifestyle, in which we are immersed in the materialistic values and behavior of worldly friends, will get us nowhere. Only frustration and inanity will be the result. Shāntideva advises us to fight shy of those whose values are contrary to the Dharma—people he habitually refers to as "those who are like children" (i.e., in terms designed to stimulate feelings of concern rather than resentment). Thus Shāntideva prescribes solitude, a flight from the world—not of course in a puritanical, world-denying sense, but in a spirit of inner freedom. Tranquillity of mind, he says significantly, is obtained "by those who *joyfully* renounce the world," by those who "never turn a backward glance." And he celebrates the idea of retreat in the wilderness in verses of extraordinary lyrical beauty.

The practice is naturally attended by difficulties and obstacles, and these are summarized under two headings: desire for companionship and desire for property. In the first case, Shāntideva addresses the question of sex and the problem posed by physical desire—which naturally leads to the practical matter of how to attenuate, and defuse, sexual obsession. As a meditative technique, he recommends to himself and to his monastic audience a reflection and concentration on the impure, unattractive aspects of women's bodies. And, not without a considerable sense of humor, he expatiates on the absurdity of the social conventions of courtship and marriage, whether viewed *sub specie aeternitatis*, or from the perspective of sheer physical realities. Shāntideva thus gives important instructions for the ordained community on how the virtue of chastity might be cultivated and the state of celibacy preserved. But as we have said, since the point at issue is physical desire as such, the teaching here is of universal application, irrespective of social status and, for that matter, sexual orientation. Lay practitioners also are obliged to recognize that in sexual life, as in other aspects of saṃsāric existence, the mind is attracted to what is in fact a mirage. It habitually functions by thoroughly ignoring objective physical realities or at any rate by being highly selective in what it notices. And in any case, desire is desire—it must be transcended if progress on the path (the tantric path included) is to be possible.

As with personal attachments, so with the acquisition of property, Shāntideva's message is the same: people spend their lives chasing chimeras. They destroy themselves in the quest for wealth which, even when acquired, is only for the enjoyment of a brief and passing moment— "Mouthfuls of the hay the oxen get as recompense for having pulled the cart!" And yet, Shāntideva exclaims, "with a millionth part of such vexation enlightenment itself could be attained! . . . "

After again extolling the advantages of solitude, Shāntideva begins to consider two themes that form the high point of his teaching and which are the essence of the bodhisattva path: meditation on the equality of self and other, and meditation on the exchange of self and other.[4] Here the subject matter becomes complex, hinging as it does on the profound doctrine of emptiness. For it quickly becomes apparent that on the bodhisattva path, compassion is seen not merely as sympathy for the sufferings of beings, or even as the resolve to do something about it in practical terms (however admirable such work may be). In Mahāyāna Buddhism, compassion involves, through the application of wisdom, the transcending of the notion of ego itself and the understanding that, in the final analysis, the existential barrier dividing self from other is totally unreal, a mere mental construction. Once this barrier has been crossed, and the bodhisattva realizes the unreality of the distinction between self and other, the suffering of others becomes as real to him as his own. Indeed, they *are* his sufferings; and the urge to relieve them, both immediately and ultimately, becomes his primary impulse. These ideas will be unfamiliar and perhaps disconcerting to many readers, and the meaning of the text itself is not always easy to understand. For this reason substantial excerpts translated from the Tibetan commentary of Khenchen Kunzang Palden have been provided by way of an appendix. It is sufficient to emphasize here that the Buddhist teachings on compassion are grounded in the wisdom of emptiness. It is from this that they derive their meaning and compelling force, their validity and at the same time their practical possibility.

> Those desiring speedily to be
> A refuge for themselves and other beings,
> Should interchange the terms of "I" and "other,"
> And thus embrace a sacred mystery. (8.120)

This exchange, fully possible only for those who have completely gone beyond the duality of self and other, is the peak of bodhisattva practice and takes us to the heart of Buddhist wisdom. This is the point from which all the teachings of *The Way of the Bodhisattva* derive their sense and find their completion. Everything is condensed into a single stanza which Shāntideva proclaims with the finality of a cosmic principle:

All the joy the world contains
Has come through wishing happiness for others.
All the misery the world contains
Has come through wanting pleasure for oneself.(8.129)

Here, as always, Shāntideva does not leave us gaping in stunned amazement. He quickly sets about with methods designed to help us on our way. In so doing he indicates a practice that, according to His Holiness the Dalai Lama, is unique in the entire range of Buddhist teaching. Directed at the principal obstacle to the realization of equality (namely the ego itself), and taking as his cue the idea of exchange, he describes a meditation that consists in projecting oneself, through a feat of sympathetic imagination, into the position of an opponent. Looking back, as it were, through the opponent's eyes, the meditator must target his or her own ego, generating the appropriate "negative" emotion of jealousy, competitive rivalry or pride, and try to get a firsthand impression of what it is like to be at the receiving end of one's own behavior. This technique, which is of great psychological interest and effectiveness, has been commented on at length by Kunzang Palden, and a translation of his remarks are found in an appendix at the end of the book. Fascinating as this technique is as a means of diminishing the ego's strength and also of attenuating the illusory barrier between self and other, it will be evident from what has been said previously that for the real experience of equality and exchange to occur, a true understanding of the wisdom of emptiness is indispensable. We can thus perceive the importance of Shāntideva's metaphysical position and appreciate the extent to which his entire teaching is inspired and underpinned by this. The *Bodhicharyāvatāra* would be incomplete without a detailed discussion of wisdom.

THE WISDOM CHAPTER

The celebrated ninth chapter on wisdom is of course daunting in its complexity. It is not easy to follow, and it is understandable perhaps that by the majority of readers it will be passed over in silence. But sooner or later, the question of wisdom and what Shāntideva means by this must be considered—as the culmination of, and also the key to, the entire bodhisattva path. Shāntideva begins by pointing out that the whole of the *Bodhicharyāvatāra* so far—all the methods for purifying the mind and generating the virtues of vigilance, patience, courage, and so on, are geared toward wisdom, the direct realization of emptiness, absolute bodhichitta, without which the true practice of compassion is impossible.

From the point of view of metaphysics, Shāntideva was an adherent of the Prāsaṅgika Mādhyamika, the Middle Way Consequence school of Buddhist philosophy. This tradition, founded by Nāgārjuna in the second century and counting among its adherents a series of incomparable masters (Āryadeva, Buddhapālita, Chandrakīrti, Shāntideva, Atīsha, and others), flowered in India uninterruptedly for over a thousand years. Transmitted to Tibet in the eighth century, it has been upheld to this day as the supreme expression of the Buddha's wisdom teachings. There is obviously no question here of giving an adequate survey of Mādhyamika thought, but perhaps the following remarks will help readers gain an idea of its main lines and basic import.[5]

In the centuries that followed the Buddha's death, various attempts were made to organize and formulate his teachings. Different systems appeared, basing themselves on the recorded scriptures, each purporting to express the Buddha's intended meaning. Four, or rather three, great syntheses emerged: that of the Vaibhāshika and Sautrāntika (which for practical purposes may be taken together), that of the Mādhyamika, and that of the Vijñānavāda (also referred to as Yogāchāra or Chittamātra, the "mind-only" school). That there should be a multiplicity of systems is not in itself surprising. From the time of his enlightenment until his death fifty years later, the Buddha bestowed his teachings for the benefit of many different audiences. The purpose of his doctrine was always the same: to liberate beings from the round of suffering. The expression of this purpose, however, differed according to the capacity of his hearers. It is therefore to be expected that the body of teachings remaining after his departure from the world should be rich and varied, containing elements that sometimes even contradict each other. The Mādhyamika deals with this state of affairs by saying that statements made by the Buddha are of two kinds: absolute (*nītārtha*), corresponding to his true meaning, as understood by himself, and expedient (*neyārtha*), corresponding to a partial expression of his meaning, geared to the understanding of his hearers, intended to lead them along the path to perfect comprehension and being therefore of provisional validity. Parallel with this division is the doctrine of the two truths: absolute truth (*paramārtha*) corresponding to reality, and relative truth (*saṃvṛiti*) corresponding to empirical experience. According to Nāgārjuna, the Buddha skillfully graduated his teaching according to pedagogical necessity. He affirmed the existence of the *ātman*, the self, as against the "nihilist" (who disbelieves in survival after death), in order to maintain the truth of karma and ethical responsibility. By contrast, he denied the existence of the ātman, as against the "eternalist" (who takes the self to be a changeless essence). He also said that there is neither self nor no-self.

What conclusion is to be drawn from this? What, according to Nāgārjuna, was Buddha's real position? We may take as our starting point Shāntideva's own words:

> Relative and absolute,
> These the two truths are declared to be.
> The absolute is not within the reach of intellect,
> For intellect is grounded in the relative. (9.2)

The meaning of this is that all statements, all theories, anything emerging from the operations of the rational intelligence, have the nature of relative truth. Theories may be of practical utility and may concur with empirical experience, but as expressions of the absolute truth, the ultimate "nature of things," they are inadequate. The absolute is suprarational and cannot be expressed in conceptual terms. Thus, in the *Majjhima Nikāya*,[6] the Buddha is recorded as saying that "the Tathāgata is free from all theories." And again, "The view that everything exists is, Kachchāyana, one extreme; that it does not exist is another. Not accepting the two extremes, the Tathāgata proclaims the truth from the middle position."[7] The second passage, also preserved in the Pāli scriptures, is referred to explicitly by Nāgārjuna in his great work, *The Stanzas on the Middle Way*, with the remark that "the Lord has rejected both views: that of 'is' and that of 'is not.' "[8] In other words, he has rejected all *views*. This means that any statement claiming to encapsulate the ultimate truth, any formulation that points to "this" or "that" as being ultimately real, is false—false for the simple reason that it is a formulation, emanating from the conceptual intelligence.

At first sight, this seems to be a form of nihilism. Apparently, it is the assertion that in the ordinary run of things we can know nothing of the truth; reality seems to be totally beyond our grasp; and Mādhyamika has not infrequently been misunderstood and criticized in this way.[9] But to say that the "absolute lies not within the realm of intellect" does not mean that it cannot be known; it means simply that it exceeds the powers of ordinary thought and verbal expression. The knowledge of the absolute transcends thought. It is suprarational. It is nonconceptual and nondual—quite different, we may suppose, from anything that we have ever experienced to date. It is *prajñā*: immediate intuitive insight into "suchness," the wisdom of emptiness beyond subject and object.

How is one to attain or even approach this kind of knowledge? Shāntideva gives the answer in a key stanza (the very point in his recitation at Nālandā when, according to the story, he and Mañjushrī began to rise into the air):

> When real and nonreal both
> Are absent from before the mind,
> Nothing else remains for mind to do
> But rest in perfect peace, from concepts free. (9.34)

These lines adumbrate the task in hand: the mind is to be left as it is, free and untrammeled, simply aware, no longer caught up and entangled in thoughts and theories and the grasping reification of self and substance. On the level of philosophical discourse, this involves the demonstration of the inadequacy of theories and systems purporting to express the ultimate truth. The basic position of Mādhyamika is that reason is insufficient. It is the recognition, in fact the discovery, that there is a radical lack in the structure of reason itself—something that prevents it from attaining to true knowledge of the absolute. In the final analysis, all rational formulations, however ingenious, contain within themselves paradox and inconsistency, the seed, in other words, of their own refutation. The task of Mādhyamika is to expose this inner incoherence. It proceeds in the knowledge that, if pushed in debate to explain themselves, all rationally constructed formulations will end in contradiction. Thus Mādhyamika does not advance a position of its own. Rather than a body of doctrines, it is primarily a method, a system of philosophical criticism. It is dialectic pure and simple. Its procedure is to take a dogmatic assertion (the doctrine of the self, the theory of causation, or the existence of a divine creator, and so on) and gradually refute it—not by coming into head-on collision by positing a contrary view, but by gradually exposing, through a series of logical steps, the theory's own inner incoherence. Ultimately the assertion is reduced to absurdity and stands revealed as unequal to its original claim. In the end, theories, all theories—Buddhist theories included—fall to the ground through sheer inanity. No intellectual construction can withstand such analysis; the purpose of Mādhyamika is to reduce to total silence the restless, questing intellect, forever condemned to one-sidedness and a specific viewpoint. A mental stillness supervenes, and conceptual elaboration is annihilated, making possible an insight that lies beyond thought construction. This prepares the ground for the experience of shūnyatā, emptiness itself.[10] The position of the Mādhyamika thus resembles the Kantian critique in modern Western philosophy, but as T. R. V. Murti suggests, it goes far beyond Kant in perceiving that criticism may itself yield wisdom and provide the ground for a spiritual path.[11]

In his account, Shāntideva surveys the range of Mādhyamika arguments as these had been played out from Nāgārjuna until his own time. The ninth chapter of the *Bodhicharyāvatāra* thus presents an encyclopedic overview, which is extremely useful for the understanding of the system itself. It devotes considerable space to the refutation of the realism of the Vaibhāṣhika and Sautrāntika schools, the belief in the ultimate existence of indivisible particles of matter and instants of consciousness. This was the prime object of Nāgārjuna's polemic. Then there is a dismantling of the ātman theory as propounded by the early Hindu Saṃkhya and a critique of the Mīmāṃsā and Nyāya schools of Indian philosophy, to which Nāgārjuna's great disciple Āryadeva devoted particular attention. This is complemented by a lengthy account of the (Buddhist) Vijñānavāda, presented and refuted in the spirit of Chandrakīrti. And throughout the chapter, and for that matter the whole of the book, Shāntideva's method of *reductio ad absurdum* (*prasaṅga*) reveals him as a true follower of Buddhapālita.[12]

Even in the earlier chapters of the *Bodhicharyāvatāra*, well before turning explicitly to metaphysical questions, it is evident that Shāntideva is constantly preoccupied with the view of emptiness and the implications of this in all aspects of the bodhisattva path. The questions he asks about the nature of mental defilements, at the end of chapter 4, and the sudden discussion of the self in chapter 6, to take just two examples, show that the philosophical perspective is always very close to the surface. And the most remarkable feature of the ninth chapter, taken within the context of the *Bodhicharyāvatāra* as a whole, is that it shows that the wisdom of emptiness is not merely relevant to bodhisattva training, it is actually indispensable. Shāntideva demonstrates that, far from being a matter of rarefied metaphysics or academic discussion, removed from the concerns of practical existence, Mādhyamika is fundamentally a vision and a way of life. It is the ultimate heart and soul of the Buddha's teaching. In the twenty or so stanzas at the end of the ninth chapter, Shāntideva shows how it is precisely the absence of this wisdom that lies at the root of saṃsāra and the sorrows of the world; and he poignantly concludes his message with verses of great beauty and pathos.

> When shall I be able to allay and quench
> The dreadful heat of suffering's blazing fires,
> With plenteous rains of my own bliss
> That pour torrential from my clouds of merit?
>
> My wealth of merit gathered in,
> With reverence but without conceptual aim,
> When shall I reveal this truth of emptiness
> To those who go to ruin through belief in substance? (9.166–167)

THE TEXT AND
THE TRANSLATION

According to tradition, *The Way of the Bodhisattva* was first translated into Tibetan in the eighth century by the Indian master Sarvajñānadeva and the Tibetan translator Kawa Peltsek, using a manuscript from Kashmir. It was later reworked during the eleventh century by the paṇḍita Dharmashribhadra and the translator Rinchen Zangpo,[13] on the basis of a manuscript and commentary from Magadha. A final revision was made by the paṇḍita Sumatikīrti and the translator Loden Sherab.

Shāntideva's text is one of the relatively few Indian Buddhist texts of which the Sanskrit original has survived. Translations from this original have been made into European languages,[14] and based on modern linguistic and textual scholarship, these are no doubt of great value. The fact, however, that Shāntideva's text has been expounded, studied, and practiced in Tibet in an unbroken tradition, from the moment of its composition until the present day, lends the Tibetan version of *The Way of the Bodhisattva* a particular authority and constitutes, in our view, an important justification for the use of it, supported by the traditional commentaries, as the original for translation into modern languages.

Shāntideva's work is one of the great tap-roots of Tibetan Bud-

dhism and has been for over a thousand years the inspiration of generation after generation of practitioners, accomplished masters, and
ordinary folk alike. In the long lineage of teachers who have transmitted
the *Bodhicharyāvatāra* down the ages, it seems appropriate to mention
in particular the nineteenth-century master Dza Patrul Rinpoche,[15] who
occupies a position of unusual importance, as a master whose influence
has been felt throughout all schools of Tibetan Buddhism in modern
times.

After studying with all the greatest teachers of his age, Patrul Rinpoche became a wandering hermit, living in caves and under forest trees.
He belonged to no monastery and owned neither house nor property.
He meditated constantly on love and compassion, which he regarded as
the foundation and heart of spiritual practice. He possessed an extraordinary memory and knew by heart an enormous number of texts and
scriptures. He taught with inspiring simplicity from the depths of profound realization, and many extraordinary stories have been told about
him. His external behavior was often eccentric and unconventional, and
his renowned kindness was offset by a facade of disconcerting fierceness.
His practice of compassion was such that people regarded him as the
very incarnation of Shāntideva himself. And at a time when many essential teachings were falling into disuse and unfamiliarity, Patrul Rinpoche
taught the *Bodhicharyāvatāra* so often that he inspired most of the commentaries written on it in the second half of the nineteenth and the
beginning of the twentieth centuries. Thanks to him, Shāntideva's work
became one of the texts most studied and practiced in the whole of
eastern Tibet. It is said that when he died, Patrul Rinpoche's possessions
consisted of the clothes he was wearing, a bowl, and a copy of the *Bodhicharyāvatāra.*[16]

Patrul Rinpoche had many disciples, who became themselves mas-
ters and accomplished practitioners of the bodhisattva path—Mipham
Rinpoche, for example, one of the greatest Tibetan scholars of the mod-
ern age, together with his disciples and the disciples of his disciples:
Khenchen Kunzang Palden, Minyak Kunzang Sönam, Shechen Gyaltsab
Rinpoche, Kangyur Rinpoche, Kunu Rinpoche, Jamyang Khyentse
Chökyi Lodrö, Dilgo Khyentse Rinpoche, His Holiness the present Dalai
Lama, to name but a few—an illustrious line that continues to this day

and under whose aegis this translation has been made. It is our sincere hope that this new translation of the *Bodhicharyāvatāra* will be of use to the English speaking world and will help to preserve the teachings that the above mentioned masters have embodied in their lives and preserved into our time.

The present version has been translated from the Tibetan following the commentary of Kunzang Palden, a master more familiarly referred to as Khenpo Kunpel. This commentary, renowned for its thoroughness, clarity, and accessibility, is the one most studied in the monasteries and centers of the Nyingma tradition. Extant translations of the text, made both from Sanskrit and Tibetan, have also been systematically consulted. This has been particularly so with regard to the translation of Louis Finot, reworked and corrected by the Padmakara Translation Group, as well as those of Stephen Batchelor and Georges Driessens. Where divergences occur in the interpretation of the more obscure passages, the difference will usually be seen to stem from the alternative interpretations of the respective commentaries used. Batchelor and Driessens, for example, followed the commentary of the celebrated medieval master Gyalse Thogme Zangpo (1295–1369).

An attempt has been made here to translate the text into verse, thus emulating the form of the original, keeping to the traditional Tibetan structure of four-line stanzas, or *shlokas*. Translation into verse, and didactic verse at that, is indeed a hazardous enterprise these days and may well invite criticism if not hostility. The intention, aside from that of imitation, has been to produce a version that might fall easily on the ear and therefore be more easily retained—imitating, if only at a great distance, the smoothness, clarity, and occasional lyricism of Shāntideva's style. Admittedly, this was an ambitious project, and the result undoubtedly displays many defects, falling far short of the desired objective. But it will have fulfilled its purpose if it contributes to a trend in the translation and perfect future rendering of Shāntideva's work—in the hands of some truly gifted, perhaps enlightened, writer. In the meantime, the reader is asked to be patient with details of the present version imposed by metrication. A certain latitude on the level of vocabulary proved necessary, in the way of variation and interpretative paraphrase. Thus, for example, "Doctrine," "Law," "Teachings," and similar terms are all alternatives for "Dharma"; "Assembly" and "Saṅgha" are used as synonyms; and so on. Many Sanskrit words have been retained, either because they are already generally familiar or because it seemed a good thing that they should become so. On the other hand, for reasons of scansion, it is very difficult to accommodate into an English line Sanskrit names or words of more than two syllables, such as Avalokiteshvara or *sambhogakāya*. Recognizable alternatives must often be found, and one is inevitably dependent on the sympathetic cooperation of the reader. This is not a word-for-word translation, even though on most occasions it follows the Tibetan closely. Rather than being a work of scholarship, its aim is to transmit the spirit of Shāntideva's work as presented in the Tibetan Buddhist tradition, and as such it is addressed principally, though not of course exclusively, to people who aspire to actualize its teachings in their daily lives.

In conclusion, the reader may be interested by the following anecdote. In 1984, the translator had the unusual privilege of a private meeting with His Holiness the Dalai Lama, who was at that time visiting England. The translator had with him a copy of the *Bodhicharyāvatāra* and took the opportunity of asking His Holiness to bless it. He did so readily, placing the book reverently to his forehead. After a moment, he turned and said, "If I have any understanding of compassion and the practice of the bodhisattva path, it is entirely on the basis of this text that I possess it."

❀ ACKNOWLEDGMENTS

The Way of the Bodhisattva was translated by Wulstan Fletcher of the Padmakara Translation Group, with the much-appreciated assistance of Helena Blankleder. The translator is grateful to the readers Steve Gethin, John Canti, Adriane and Geoffrey Gunther, and Christopher Moore. As always, our work was entirely dependent on the help and guidance of our teachers. We are utterly indebted to Taklung Tsetrul Rinpoche, Tulku Pema Wangyal, for his inspiration, his teaching, and his example, and most especially to Jigme Khyentse Rinpoche, who transmitted the entire text, who oversaw the project from its beginning to its completion, and who through his learning and acuity, tireless support, patient help, and gentle humor has made this translation possible.

THE WAY

OF THE

BODHISATTVA

The Excellence of Bodhichitta

Homage to all buddhas and bodhisattvas.

1. To those who go in bliss,[17] the Dharma[18] they have mastered, and
     to all their heirs,[19]
   To all who merit veneration, I bow down.
   According to tradition, I shall now in brief describe
   The entrance to the bodhisattva discipline.

2. What I have to say has all been said before,
   And I am destitute of learning and of skill with words.
   I therefore have no thought that this might be of benefit to others;
   I wrote it only to sustain my understanding.

3. My faith will thus be strengthened for a little while,
   That I might grow accustomed to this virtuous way.
   But others who now chance upon my words,
   May profit also, equal to myself in fortune.

4. So hard to find such ease and wealth[20]
   Whereby to render meaningful this human birth!
   If now I fail to turn it to my profit,
   How could such a chance be mine again?

5.   As when a flash of lightning rends the night,
And in its glare shows all the dark black clouds had hid,
Likewise rarely, through the buddhas' power,
Virtuous thoughts rise, brief and transient, in the world.

6.   Thus behold the utter frailty of goodness!
Except for perfect bodhichitta,
There is nothing able to withstand
The great and overwhelming strength of evil.

7.   The mighty buddhas, pondering for many ages,
Have seen that this, and only this, will save
The boundless multitudes,
And bring them easily to supreme joy.

8.   Those who wish to overcome the sorrows of their lives,
And put to flight the pain and sufferings of beings,
Those who wish to win such great beatitude,
Should never turn their back on bodhichitta.

9.   Should bodhichitta come to birth
In one who suffers in the dungeons of saṃsāra,
In that instant he is called the buddhas' heir,
Worshipful alike to gods and men.

10.   For like the supreme substance of the alchemists,
It takes the impure form of human flesh
And makes of it the priceless body of a buddha.
Such is bodhichitta: we should grasp it firmly!

11.   If the perfect leaders of all migrant beings
Have with boundless wisdom seen its priceless worth,
We who wish to leave our nomad wandering
Should hold well to this precious bodhichitta.

12. All other virtues, like the plantain tree,[21]
    Produce their fruit, but then their force is spent.
    Alone the marvelous tree of bodhichitta
    Will bear its fruit and grow unceasingly.

13. As though they pass through perils guarded by a hero,
    Even those weighed down with dreadful wickedness
    Will instantly be freed through having bodhichitta.
    Who then would not place his trust in it?

14. Just as by the fires at the end of time,
    Great sins are utterly consumed by bodhichitta.
    Thus its benefits are boundless,
    As the Wise and Loving Lord explained to Sudhana.[22]

15. Bodhichitta, the awakening mind,
    In brief is said to have two aspects:
    First, aspiring, *bodhichitta in intention*;
    Then, *active bodhichitta*, practical engagement.

16. Wishing to depart and setting out upon the road,
    This is how the difference is conceived.
    The wise and learned thus should understand
    This difference, which is ordered and progressive.

17. *Bodhichitta in intention* bears rich fruit
    For those still wandering in saṃsāra.
    And yet a ceaseless stream of merit does not flow from it;
    For this will rise alone from *active bodhichitta*.

18. For when, with irreversible intent,
    The mind embraces bodhichitta,
    Willing to set free the endless multitudes of beings,
    At that instant, from that moment on,

19. A great and unremitting stream,
    A strength of wholesome merit,
    Even during sleep and inattention,
    Rises equal to the vastness of the sky.

20. This the Tathāgata,[23]
    In the sūtra Subāhu requested,[24]
    Said with reasoned demonstration,
    Teaching those inclined to lesser paths.

21. If with kindly generosity
    One merely has the wish to soothe
    The aching heads of other beings,
    Such merit knows no bounds.

22. No need to speak, then, of the wish
    To drive away the endless pain
    Of each and every living being,
    Bringing them unbounded virtues.

23. Could our fathers or our mothers
    Ever have so generous a wish?
    Do the very gods, the ṛiṣhis,[25] even Brahmā[26]
    Harbor such benevolence as this?

24. For in the past they never,
    Even in their dreams, conceived
    Such profit even for themselves.
    How could they have such aims for others' sake?

25. For beings do not wish their own true good,
    So how could they intend such good for others' sake?
    This state of mind so precious and so rare
    Arises truly wondrous, never seen before.

26. The pain-dispelling draft,
    This cause of joy for those who wander through the world—
    This precious attitude, this jewel of mind,
    How shall it be gauged or quantified?

27. For if the simple thought to be of help to others
    Exceeds in worth the worship of the buddhas,
    What need is there to speak of actual deeds
    That bring about the weal and benefit of beings?

28. For beings long to free themselves from misery,
    But misery itself they follow and pursue.
    They long for joy, but in their ignorance
    Destroy it, as they would a hated enemy.

29. But those who fill with bliss
    All beings destitute of joy,
    Who cut all pain and suffering away
    From those weighed down with misery,

30. Who drive away the darkness of their ignorance—
    What virtue could be matched with theirs?
    What friend could be compared to them?
    What merit is there similar to this?

31. If they who do some good, in thanks
    For favors once received, are praised,
    Why need we speak of bodhisattvas—
    Those who freely benefit the world?

32. Those who, scornfully with condescension,
    Give, just once, a single meal to others—
    Feeding them for only half a day—
    Are honored by the world as virtuous.

33. What need is there to speak of those
     Who constantly bestow on boundless multitudes
     The peerless joy of blissful buddhahood,
     The ultimate fulfillment of their hopes?

34. And those who harbor evil in their minds
     Against such lords of generosity, the Buddha's heirs,
     Will stay in hell, the Mighty One has said,
     For ages equal to the moments of their malice.

35. By contrast, good and virtuous thoughts
     Will yield abundant fruits in greater measure.
     Even in adversity, the bodhisattvas
     Never bring forth evil—only an increasing stream of goodness.

36. To them in whom this precious sacred mind
     Is born—to them I bow!
     I go for refuge in that source of happiness
     That brings its very enemies to perfect bliss.

Confession[27]

1.   To the buddhas, those thus gone,
     And to the sacred Law, immaculate, supreme, and rare,
     And to the Buddha's offspring, oceans of good qualities,
     That I might gain this precious attitude, I make a perfect offering.

2.   I offer every fruit and flower
     And every kind of healing medicine;
     And all the precious things the world affords,
     With all pure waters of refreshment;

3.   Every mountain, rich and filled with jewels;
     All sweet and lonely forest groves;
     The trees of heaven, garlanded with blossom,
     And branches heavy, laden with their fruit;

4.   The perfumed fragrance of the realms of gods and men;
     All incense, wishing trees, and trees of gems;
     All crops that grow without the tiller's care
     And every sumptuous object worthy to be offered;

5.   Lakes and meres adorned with lotuses,
     All plaintive with the sweet-voiced cries of water birds
     And lovely to the eyes, and all things wild and free,
     Stretching to the boundless limits of the sky;

6.   I hold them all before my mind, and to the supreme buddhas
       And their heirs will make a perfect gift of them.
       O, think of me with love, compassionate lords;
       Sacred objects of my prayers, accept these offerings.

7.   For I am empty-handed, destitute of merit,
       I have no other wealth. But you, protectors,
       You whose thoughts are for the good of others,
       In your great power, accept this for my sake.

8.   The buddhas and their bodhisattva children—
       I offer them myself throughout my lives.
       Supreme courageous ones, accept me totally.
       For with devotion I will be your servant.

9.   For if you will accept me, I will be
       A benefit to all, and freed from fear.
       I'll go beyond the evils of my past,
       And ever after turn my face from them.

10.   A bathing chamber excellently fragrant,
       With floors of crystal, radiant and clear,
       With graceful pillars shimmering with gems,
       All hung about with gleaming canopies of pearls—

11.   There the blissful buddhas and their heirs
       I'll bathe with many a precious vase,
       Abrim with water, sweet and pleasant,
       All to frequent strains of melody and song.

12.   With cloths of unexampled quality,
       With peerless, perfumed towels I will dry them
       And offer splendid scented clothes,
       Well dyed and of surpassing excellence.

13.   With different garments, light and supple,
And a hundred beautiful adornments,
I will grace sublime Samantabhadra,[28]
Mañjughoṣha, Lokeshvara, and their kin.

14.   And with a sumptuous fragrance that
Pervades a thousand million worlds,
I will anoint the bodies of the buddhas,
Light and gleaming bright, like pure and burnished gold.

15.   I will place before the Buddha, perfect object of my worship,
Flowers like the lotus and the mandārava,
Utpala, and other scented blossoms,
Worked and twined in lovely scented garlands.

16.   I will offer swelling clouds of incense,
Whose ambient perfume ravishes the mind,
And various foods and every kind of drink,
All delicacies worthy of the gods.

17.   I will offer precious lamps,
All perfectly contrived as golden lotuses,
A bed of flower petals scattering
Upon the level, incense-sprinkled ground.

18.   I will offer palaces immense and resonant with song,
All decked with precious pearls and pendant gems,
Gleaming treasures fit to ornament the amplitude of space:
All this I offer to the loving bodhisattvas.

19.   Precious parasols adorned with golden shafts
And bordered all around with jeweled fringes,
Upright, well-proportioned, pleasing to the eye,
Again, all this I give to all the buddhas.

20. May a multitude of other offerings,
     Accompanied by music sweet to hear,
     Be made in great successive clouds,
     To soothe the sufferings of living beings.

21. May rains of flowers, every precious thing,
     Fall down in an unceasing stream
     Upon the jewels[29] of sacred Dharma,
     The Triple Gem and all supports for offering.

22. Just as Mañjughoṣha, gentle and melodious,
     Made offerings to all the conquerors,
     Likewise I will make oblation
     To the buddhas and their bodhisattva children.

23. I will offer prayers by every way and means
     To these vast oceans of good qualities.
     May clouds of tuneful praise
     Ascend unceasingly before them.

24. To buddhas of the past, the present, and all future time,
     And to the Doctrine and Sublime Assembly,
     With bodies many as the grains of dust
     Upon the ground, I will prostrate and bow.[30]

25. To shrines and all supports
     Of bodhichitta I bow down:
     All abbots who transmit the vows, all learned masters,
     And all noble ones who practice Dharma.

26. Until the essence of enlightenment is reached,
     I go for refuge to the buddhas.
     Also I take refuge in the Doctrine
     And all the host of bodhisattvas.[31]

Confession

27. To perfect buddhas and bodhisattvas,
     In all directions, where they may reside,
     To them who are the sovereigns of great mercy,
     I press my palms together, praying thus:

28. "In this and all my other lifetimes,
     Wandering in the round without beginning,
     Blindly I have brought forth wickedness,
     Inciting others to commit the same.

29. "I have taken pleasure in such evil,
     Tricked and overmastered by my ignorance.
     Now I see the blame of it, and in my heart,
     O great protectors, I declare it!

30. "Whatever I have done against the Triple Gem,
     Against my parents, teachers, and the rest,
     Through force of my defilements,
     By the faculties of body, speech, and mind;

31. "All the evil I, a sinner, have committed,
     The sin that clings to me through many evil deeds;
     All the frightful things that I have caused to be,
     I openly declare to you, the teachers of the world.

32. "Before my evil has been cleansed away,
     It may be that my death will come to me.
     And so that, come what may, I might be freed,
     I pray you, quickly grant me your protection!"

33. The wanton Lord of Death we can't predict,
     And life's tasks done or still to do, we cannot stay.
     And whether ill or well, we cannot trust
     Our lives, our fleeting, momentary lives.

34.   And we must pass away, forsaking all.
      But I, devoid of understanding,
      Have, for sake of friend and foe alike,
      Provoked and brought about so many evils.

35.   My enemies at length will cease to be;
      My friends, and I myself
      Will cease to be;
      And all is likewise destined for destruction.

36.   All that I possess and use
      Is like the fleeting vision of a dream.
      It fades into the realms of memory;
      And fading, will be seen no more.

37.   And even in the brief course of this present life,
      So many friends and foes have passed away,
      Because of whom, the evils I have done
      Still lie, unbearable, before me.

38.   The thought came never to my mind
      That I too am a brief and passing thing.
      And so, through hatred, lust, and ignorance,
      I've been the cause of many evils.

39.   Never halting, night or day,
      My life is slipping, slipping by.
      And nothing that has passed can be regained—
      And what but death could be my destiny?

40.   There I'll be, prostrate upon my bed,
      And all around, the ones I know and love—
      But I alone shall be the one to feel
      The cutting of the thread of life.

41. And when the vanguard of the Deadly King[32] has gripped me,
     What help to me will be my friends or kin?
     For only goodness gained in life will help me:
     This, alas, is what I shrugged away.

42. O protectors! I, so little heeding,
     Had hardly guessed at horror such as this—
     And all for this brief, transient existence,
     Have gathered so much evil to myself.

43. The day they take him to the scaffold,
     Where his body will be torn and butchered,
     A man is changed, transfigured by his fear:
     His mouth is dry, his eyes start from his brow.

44. If so it is, then how will be my misery
     When stricken down, beside myself with fear,
     I see the fiend, the messenger of Death,
     Who turns on me his fell and dreadful gaze?

45. Who can save me, who can now protect me
     From this horror, from this frightful dread?
     And then I'll search the four directions,
     Seeking help, with panic-stricken eyes.

46. Nowhere help or refuge will be found.
     And sunk beneath the weight of sorrow,
     Naked, helpless, unprotected—
     What, when this befalls me, shall I do?

47. Thus from this day forth I go for refuge
     To buddhas, guardians of wandering beings,
     Who labor for the good of all that lives,
     Those mighty ones who scatter every fear.

48. In the Dharma that resides within their hearts,
    That scatters all the terrors of saṃsāra,
    And in the multitude of bodhisattvas,
    Likewise I will perfectly take refuge.

49. Gripped by dread, beside myself with terror,
    To Samantabhadra I will give myself;
    And to Mañjushrī, the melodious and gentle,
    I will give myself entirely.

50. To him whose loving deeds are steadfast,
    O my guardian, Avalokita,
    I cry out from depths of misery,
    "Protect me now, the sinner that I am!"

51. Now to the noble one, Ākāshagarbha,[33]
    And to Kṣhitigarbha, from my heart I call.
    And all protectors, great, compassionate,
    To them I go in search of refuge.

52. And to Vajrapāṇi,[34] holder of the diamond,
    The very sight of whom will rout
    All dangers like the deadly host of Yama;
    To him indeed I fly for safety.

53. Formerly your words I have transgressed,
    But now I see these terrors all around.
    To you indeed I come for help,
    And pray you, swiftly save me from this fear.

54. For if, alarmed by common ills,
    I act according to the doctor's words,
    What need to speak of when I'm constantly brought low
    By lust and all the hundred other torments?

55. And if, by one of these alone,
     The dwellers in the world are all thrown down,
     And if no other remedy exists,
     No other healing elsewhere to be found

56. Than words of the omniscient physician,
     Uprooting every ill and suffering,
     The thought to turn on him deaf ears
     Is raving folly, wretched and contemptible.

57. If along a small and ordinary cliff
     I need to pick my way with special care,
     What need to speak of the immense crevasse
     That plunges down, unnumbered fathoms deep?

58. "Today, at least, I shall not die,"
     So rash to lull myself with words like these!
     My dissolution and my hour of death
     Will come upon me ineluctably.

59. So why am I so unafraid,
     For what escape is there for me?
     Death, my death will certainly come round,
     So how can I relax in careless ease?

60. Of life's experience, all seasons past,
     What's left to me, what now remains?
     By clinging to what now is here no more,
     My teacher's precepts I have disobeyed.

61. This span of life and all that it contains,
     My kith and kin are all to be abandoned!
     I must leave them, setting out alone,
     What grounds are there for telling friend from foe?[35]

62. And therefore how can I make sure
    To rid myself of evil, only cause of sorrow?
    This should be my one concern,
    My only thought both night and day.

63. Therefore all the sins I have committed,
    Blinded in the dark of ignorance:
    Actions evil by their nature
    Or the faults of broken vows,[36]

64. Mindful of the suffering to come,
    I join my palms and ceaselessly prostrate,
    And all my evils I will now confess
    Directly in the presence of the buddhas.

65. I pray you, guides and guardians of the world,
    To take me as I am, a sinful man.
    And all these actions, evil as they are,
    I promise I will never do again.

Commitment

1.   With joy I celebrate
   The virtue that relieves all beings
   From the sorrows of the states of loss,[37]
   And places those who languish in the realms of bliss.

2.   And I rejoice in virtue that creates the cause
   Of gaining the enlightened state,
   And celebrate the freedom won
   By living beings from the round of pain.

3.   And in the buddhahood of the protectors I delight
   And in the stages[38] of the buddhas' offspring.

4.   The intention, ocean of great good,
   That seeks to place all beings in the state of bliss,
   And every action for the benefit of all:
   Such is my delight and all my joy.

5.   And so I join my hands and pray
   The buddhas who reside in every quarter:
   Kindle now the Dharma's light
   For those who grope, bewildered, in the dark of suffering!

6. I join my hands, beseeching the enlightened ones
    Who wish to pass beyond the bonds of sorrow:
    Do not leave us in our ignorance;
    Remain among us for unnumbered ages!

7. And through these actions now performed,[39]
    By all the virtue I have just amassed,
    May all the pain of every living being
    Be wholly scattered and destroyed!

8. For all those ailing in the world,
    Until their every sickness has been healed,
    May I myself become for them
    The doctor, nurse, the medicine itself.

9. Raining down a flood of food and drink,
    May I dispel the ills of thirst and famine.
    And in the ages marked by scarcity and want,[40]
    May I myself appear as drink and sustenance.

10. For sentient beings, poor and destitute,
    May I become a treasure ever plentiful,
    And lie before them closely in their reach,
    A varied source of all that they might need.

11. My body, thus, and all my goods besides,
    And all my merits gained and to be gained,
    I give them all away withholding nothing
    To bring about the benefit of beings.

12. Nirvāṇa is attained by giving all,
    Nirvāṇa the objective of my striving.
    Everything therefore must be abandoned,
    And it is best to give it all to others.

13. This body I have given up
    To serve the pleasure of all living beings.
    Let them kill and beat and slander it,
    And do to it whatever they desire.

14. And though they treat it like a toy,
    Or make of it the butt of every mockery,
    My body has been given up to them—
    There's no use, now, to make so much of it.

15. And so let beings do to me
    Whatever does not bring them injury.
    Whenever they catch sight of me,
    Let this not fail to bring them benefit.

16. If those who see me entertain
    A thought of anger or devotion,
    May these states supply the cause
    Whereby their good and wishes are fulfilled.

17. All those who slight me to my face,
    Or do me any other evil,
    Even if they blame or slander me,
    May they attain the fortune of enlightenment!

18. May I be a guard for those who are protectorless,
    A guide for those who journey on the road.
    For those who wish to go across the water,
    May I be a boat, a raft, a bridge.

19. May I be an isle for those who yearn for landfall,
    And a lamp for those who long for light;
    For those who need a resting place, a bed;
    For all who need a servant, may I be their slave.

20. May I be the wishing jewel, the vase of plenty,
    A word of power and the supreme healing;
    May I be the tree of miracles,
    And for every being the abundant cow.

21. Like the earth and the pervading elements,
    Enduring as the sky itself endures,
    For boundless multitudes of living beings,
    May I be their ground and sustenance.

22. Thus for every thing that lives,
    As far as are the limits of the sky,
    May I provide their livelihood and nourishment
    Until they pass beyond the bonds of suffering.

23. Just as all the buddhas of the past
    Embraced the awakened attitude of mind,
    And in the precepts of the bodhisattvas
    Step by step abode and trained,

24. Just so, and for the benefit of beings,
    I will also have this attitude of mind,
    And in those precepts, step by step,
    I will abide and train myself.

25. That this most pure and spotless state of mind
    Might be embraced and constantly increase,
    The prudent who have cultivated it
    Should praise it highly in such words as these:

26. "Today my life has given fruit.
    This human state has now been well assumed.
    Today I take my birth in Buddha's line,
    And have become the buddhas' child and heir.

27. "In every way, then, I will undertake
    Activities befitting such a rank.
    And I will do no act to mar
    Or compromise this high and faultless lineage.

28. "For I am like a blind man who has found
    A precious gem within a mound of filth.
    Exactly so, as if by some strange chance,
    The enlightened mind has come to birth in me.

29.   "This is the draft of immortality,
That slays the Lord of Death, the slaughterer of beings,
The rich unfailing treasure-mine
To heal the poverty of wanderers.

30.   "It is the sovereign remedy,
That perfectly allays all maladies.
It is the wishing tree bestowing rest
On those who wander wearily the pathways of existence.

31.   "It is the universal vehicle that saves
All wandering beings from the states of loss—
The rising moon of the enlightened mind
That soothes the sorrows born of the afflictions.

32.   "It is a mighty sun that utterly dispels
The gloom and ignorance of wandering beings,
The creamy butter, rich and full,
All churned from milk of holy Teaching.

33.   "Living beings! Wayfarers upon life's paths,
Who wish to taste the riches of contentment,
Here before you is the supreme bliss—
Here, O ceaseless wanderers, is your fulfillment!

34.   "And so, within the sight of all protectors,
I summon every being, calling them to buddhahood—
And till that state is reached, to every earthly joy!
May gods and demigods, and all the rest, rejoice!"

Awareness

1.   The children of the Conqueror who thus
Have firmly grasped this bodhichitta
Should never turn aside from it
But always strive to keep its disciplines.

2.   Whatever was begun without due heed,
And all that was not properly conceived,
Although a promise and a pledge were given,
It is right to hesitate—to press on or draw back.

3.   Yet all the buddhas and their heirs
Have thought of this in their great wisdom;
I myself have weighed and pondered it,
So why should I now doubt and hesitate?

4.   For if I bind myself with promises,
But fail to carry out my words in deed,
Then every being will have been betrayed.
What destiny must lie in store for me?

5.   If in the teachings it is said
That one who in his thought intends
To give away a little thing but then draws back
Will take rebirth among the hungry ghosts,

6. How can I expect a happy destiny
   If from my heart I summon
   Wandering beings to the highest bliss,
   But then deceive and let them down?

7. And as for those who, losing bodhichitta,
   Nonetheless attain to liberation,
   This is through the inconceivable effect of karma,
   Only understood by the Omniscient.[41]

8. This failure is indeed the gravest
   Of all bodhisattva downfalls.
   For should it ever come to pass,
   The good of every being is cast down.

9. And anyone who, for a single instant,
   Halts the merit of a bodhisattva
   Will wander endlessly in states of misery,
   Because the welfare of all beings is brought low.

10. Destroy a single being's joy
    And you will work the ruin of yourself.
    But if the happiness of all is brought to nothing . . .
    What need is there to speak of this?

11. And one who wanders in saṃsāra,
    Who time and time again embraces bodhichitta,
    Only to destroy it through his faults,
    Will long be barred from bodhisattva grounds.

12. Therefore I will act devotedly
    According to the promise I have made.
    For if I fail thus to apply myself,
    I'll fall from low to even lower states.

13. Striving for the benefit of all that lives,
    Unnumbered buddhas have already lived and passed,
    But I, by virtue of my sins, have failed
    To come within the compass of their healing works.[42]

14. And this will always be my lot
    If I continue to behave like this,
    And I will suffer pains and bondage,
    Wounds and laceration in the lower realms.

15. The appearance of the buddhas in the world,
    True faith and the attainment of the human form,
    An aptitude for good: all these are rare.
    And when will all this come to me again?

16. Today, indeed, I'm hale and hearty,
    Have enough to eat, and am without affliction.
    And yet this life is fleeting and deceptive.
    This body is but briefly lent to me.

17. And yet the way I act is such
    That I shall not regain a human life!
    And losing this, my precious human form,
    My evils will be many, virtues none.[43]

18. Here is now the chance for wholesome deeds,
    But if I fail now to accomplish virtue,
    What will be my lot, what shall I do,
    When trapped in lower realms, enmeshed in misery?

19. Never, there, performing any virtue,
    Only ever perpetrating evil,
    Thus for a hundred million aeons,
    Happy states[44] will never come to me.

20. This is why Lord Buddha has declared
     That like a turtle that perchance can place
     Its head within a yoke adrift upon a shoreless sea,
     This human birth is difficult to find!

21. If evil acts of but a single instant
     Lead to deepest hell for many ages,
     The evils I have done from time without beginning—
     No need to say that they will keep me from the states of bliss!

22. And mere experience of such pain
     Does not result in being freed from it.
     For in the very suffering of such states,
     More evil will occur, and then in great abundance.

23. Thus, having found reprieve from all these things,
     If I now fail to train myself in virtue,
     What greater folly could there ever be?
     How more could I betray myself?

24. And though all this I understand,
     But later waste my time in foolish idleness,
     Then when my time to die comes round,
     My sorrows will be black indeed.

25. And when my body burns so long
     In fires of hell so unendurable,
     My mind likewise will also be tormented—
     Burned in flames of infinite regret.

26. For it's as if by chance that I have gained
     This state so hard to find, wherein to help myself.
     And now, when freedom—power of choice—is mine,
     If once again I'm led away to hell,

27.   I am as if benumbed by sorcery,
       My mind reduced to total impotence
       With no perception of the madness overwhelming me.
       O what is it that has me in its grip?

28.   Anger, lust—these enemies of mine—
       Are limbless and devoid of faculties.
       They have no bravery, no cleverness;
       How then have they reduced me to such slavery?

29.   I it is who welcome them within my heart,
       Allowing them to harm me at their pleasure!
       I who suffer all without resentment—
       Thus my abject patience, all displaced!

30.   If all the gods and demigods besides
       Together came against me as my foes,
       Their mighty strength—all this would not avail
       To fling me in the fires of deepest hell.

31.   And yet, the mighty fiend of my afflictions,
       Flings me in an instant headlong down
       To where the mighty lord of mountains[45]
       Would be burned, its very ashes all consumed.

32.   No other enemy indeed
       Has lived so long as my defiled emotions—
       O my enemy, afflictive passion,
       Endless and beginningless companion!

33.   All other foes that I appease and wait upon
       Will show me favors, give me every aid,
       But should I serve my dark defiled emotions,
       They will only harm me, draw me down to grief.

34. Therefore, if these long-lived, ancient enemies of mine,
    The wellspring only of increasing woe,
    Can find their lodging safe within my heart,
    What joy or peace in this world can be found?

35. And if the jail guards of the prisons of saṃsāra,
    The butchers and tormentors of infernal realms,
    All lurk within me in the web of craving,
    What joy can ever be my destiny?

36. I will not leave the fight until, before my eyes,
    These enemies of mine are all destroyed.
    For if, aroused to fury by the merest slight,
    Incapable of sleep until the scores are settled,

37. Foolish rivals, both to suffer when they die,
    Will draw the battle lines and do their best to win,
    And careless of the pain of cut and thrust,
    Will stand their ground, refusing to give way,

38. No need to say that I will not lose heart,
    Regardless of the hardships of the fray.
    These natural foes today I'll strive to crush—
    These enemies, the source of all my pain.

39. The wounds inflicted by the enemy in futile wars
    Are flaunted by the soldier as a trophy.
    So in the high endeavor for so great a prize,
    Why should hurt and injury dismay me?

40. When fishers, butchers, farmers, and the like,
    Intending just to gain their livelihood,
    Will suffer all the miseries of heat and cold,
    How can I not bear the same to gain the happiness of beings?

41.　When I pledged myself to free from their affliction
　　　Beings who abide in every region,
　　　Stretching to the limits of the sky,
　　　I myself was subject to the same afflictions.

42.　Thus I did not have the measure of my strength—
　　　To speak like this was clear insanity.
　　　More reason, then, for never drawing back,
　　　Abandoning the fight against defiled confusion.[46]

43.　This shall be my all-consuming passion;
　　　Filled with rancor I will wage my war!
　　　Though this emotion seems to be defiled,
　　　It halts defilement and shall not be spurned.

44.　Better if I perish in the fire,
　　　Better that my head be severed from my body
　　　Than ever I should serve or reverence
　　　My mortal foes, defiled emotions.

45.　Common enemies, when driven from the state,
　　　Retreat and base themselves in other lands,
　　　And muster all their strength the better to return.
　　　But our afflictions are without such strategems.

46.　Defiled emotions, scattered by the eye of wisdom!
　　　Where will you now run, when driven from my mind?
　　　Whence would you return to do me harm?
　　　But oh—my mind is feeble. I am indolent!

47.　And yet defilements are not in the object,
　　　Nor yet within the faculties, nor somewhere in between.
　　　And if not elsewhere, where is their abode
　　　Whence they might wreak their havoc on the world?
　　　They are simple mirages, and so—take heart!
　　　Banish all your fear and strive to know their nature.
　　　Why suffer needlessly the pains of hell?

48. This is how I should reflect and labor,
    Taking up the precepts just set forth.
    What invalid in need of medicine
    Ignored his doctor's words and gained his health?

Vigilance

1. Those who wish to keep a rule of life
   Must guard their minds in perfect self-possession.
   Without this guard upon the mind,
   No discipline can ever be maintained.

2. Wandering where it will, the elephant of mind,
   Will bring us down to pains of deepest hell.
   No worldly beast, however wild,
   Could bring upon us such calamities.

3. If, with mindfulness' rope,
   The elephant of the mind is tethered all around,
   Our fears will come to nothing,
   Every virtue drop into our hands.

4. Tigers, lions, elephants, and bears,
   Snakes and every hostile beast,
   Those who guard the prisoners in hell,
   All ghosts and ghouls and every evil phantom,

5. By simple binding of this mind alone,
   All these things are likewise bound.
   By simple taming of this mind alone,
   All these things are likewise tamed.

6.   For all anxiety and fear,
     All sufferings in boundless measure,
     Their source and wellspring is the mind itself,
     Thus the Truthful One has said.

7.   The hellish whips to torture living beings—
     Who has made them and to what intent?
     Who has forged this burning iron ground;
     Whence have all these demon women sprung?[47]

8.   All are but the offspring of the sinful mind,
     Thus the Mighty One has said.
     Thus throughout the triple world[48]
     There is no greater bane than mind itself.

9.   If transcendent giving is
     To dissipate the poverty of beings,
     In what way, since the poor are always with us,
     Have former buddhas practiced perfect generosity?

10.   The true intention to bestow on every being
     All possessions—and the fruits of such a gift:
     By such, the teachings say, is generosity perfected.
     And this, as we may see, is but the mind itself.

11.   Where, indeed, could beings, fishes, and the rest
     Be placed, to shield them totally from suffering?
     Deciding to refrain from harming them
     Is said to be perfection of morality.

12.   The hostile multitudes are vast as space—
     What chance is there that all should be subdued?
     Let but this angry mind be overthrown
     And every foe is then and there destroyed.

13. To cover all the earth with sheets of hide—
     Where could such amounts of skin be found?
     But simply wrap some leather round your feet,
     And it's as if the whole earth had been covered!

14. Likewise, we can never take
     And turn aside the outer course of things.
     But only seize and discipline the mind itself,
     And what is there remaining to be curbed?

15. A clear intent can fructify
     And bring us birth in lofty Brahmā's realm.
     The acts of body and of speech are less—
     They do not generate a like result.

16. Recitations and austerities,
     Long though they may prove to be,
     If practiced with distracted mind,
     Are futile, so the Knower of the Truth has said.

17. All who fail to know and penetrate
     This secret of the mind, the Dharma's peak,
     Although they wish for joy and sorrow's end,
     Will wander uselessly in misery.

18. This is so, and therefore I will seize
     This mind of mine and guard it well.
     What use to me so many harsh austerities?
     But let me only discipline and guard my mind!

19. When in wild, unruly crowds
     We move with care to shield our broken limbs,
     Likewise when we live in evil company,
     Our wounded minds we should not fail to guard.

20. For if I carefully protect my wounds
    Because I fear the hurt of cuts and bruises,
    Why should I not guard my wounded mind,
    For fear of being crushed beneath the cliffs of hell?[49]

21. If this is how I act and live,
    Then even in the midst of evil folk,
    Or even with fair women, all is well.
    My diligent observance of the vows will not decline.

22. Let my property and honor all grow less,
    And likewise all my health and livelihood,
    And even other virtues—all can go!
    But never will I disregard my mind.

23. All you who would protect your minds,
    Maintain awareness and your mental vigilance.
    Guard them both, at cost of life and limb—
    Thus I join my hands, beseeching you.

24. Those disabled by ill health
    Are helpless, powerless to act.
    The mind, when likewise cramped by ignorance,
    Is impotent and cannot do its work.

25. And those who have no mental vigilance,
    Though they may hear the teachings, ponder them or meditate,
    With minds like water seeping from a leaking jug,
    Their learning will not settle in their memories.

26. Many have devotion, perseverance,
    Are learned also and endowed with faith,
    But through the fault of lacking mental vigilance,
    Will not escape the stain of sin and downfall.

27. Lack of vigilance is like a thief
    Who slinks behind when mindfulness abates.
    And all the merit we have gathered in
    He steals, and down we go to lower realms.

28. Defilements are a band of robbers
    Waiting for their chance to bring us injury.
    They steal our virtue, when their moment comes,
    And batter out the life of happy destinies.

29. Therefore, from the gateway of awareness
    Mindfulness shall not have leave to stray.
    And if it wanders, it shall be recalled,
    By thoughts of anguish in the lower worlds.

30. In those endowed with fortune and devotion,
    Mindfulness is cultivated easily—
    Through fear, and by the counsels of their abbots,
    And staying ever in their teacher's company.

31. The buddhas and the bodhisattvas both
    Possess unclouded vision, seeing everything:
    Everything lies open to their gaze,
    And likewise I am always in their presence.

32. One who has such thoughts as these
    Will gain devotion and a sense of fear and shame.
    For such a one, the memory of Buddha
    Rises frequently before the mind.

33. When mindfulness is stationed as a sentinel,
    A guard upon the threshold of the mind,
    Mental scrutiny is likewise present,
    Returning when forgotten or dispersed.

34. If at the outset, when I check my mind,
    I find within some fault or insufficiency,
    I'll stay unmoving, like a log,
    In self-possession and determination.

35. I shall never, vacantly,
    Allow my gaze to wander all about,
    But rather with a focused mind
    Will always go with eyes cast down.

36. But that I might relax my gaze,
    I'll sometimes raise my eyes and look around.
    And if some person stands within my sight,
    I'll greet him with a friendly word of welcome.

37. And yet, to spy the dangers on the road,
    I'll scrutinize the four directions one by one.
    And when I stop to rest, I'll turn my head
    And look behind me, back along my path.

38. And so, I'll spy the land, in front, behind,
    To see if I should go or else return.
    And thus in every situation,
    I shall know my needs and act accordingly.

39. Deciding on a given course,
    Determining the actions of my body,
    From time to time I'll verify
    My body's actions, by repeated scrutiny.

40. This mind of mine, a wild and rampant elephant,
    I'll tether to that sturdy post: reflection on the Teaching.
    And I shall narrowly stand guard
    That it might never slip its bonds and flee.

41. Those who strive to master concentration
     Should never for an instant be distracted.
     They should constantly investigate themselves,
     Examining the movements of their minds.

42. In fearful situations, times of celebration,
     One may desist, when self-survey becomes impossible.
     For it is taught that in the times of generosity,
     The rules of discipline may be suspended.

43. When something has been planned and started on,
     Attention should not drift to other things.
     With thoughts fixed on the chosen target,
     That and that alone should be pursued.

44. Behaving in this way, all tasks are well performed,
     And nothing is achieved by doing otherwise.
     Afflictions, the reverse of vigilance,
     Can never multiply if this is how you act.

45. And if by chance you must take part
     In lengthy conversations worthlessly,
     Or if you come upon sensational events,
     Then cast aside delight and taste for them.

46. If you find you're grubbing in the soil,
     Or pulling up the grass or tracing idle patterns on the ground,
     Remembering the teachings of the Blissful One,
     In fear, restrain yourself at once.

47. When you feel the wish to walk about,
     Or even to express yourself in speech,
     First examine what is in your mind.
     For they will act correctly who have stable minds.

48. When the urge arises in the mind
To feelings of desire or wrathful hate,
Do not act! Be silent, do not speak!
And like a log of wood be sure to stay.

49. When the mind is wild with mockery
And filled with pride and haughty arrogance,
And when you want to show the hidden faults of others,
To bring up old dissensions or to act deceitfully,

50. And when you want to fish for praise,
Or criticize and spoil another's name,
Or use harsh language, sparring for a fight,
It's then that like a log you should remain.

51. And when you yearn for wealth, attention, fame,
A circle of admirers serving you,
And when you look for honors, recognition—
It's then that like a log you should remain.

52. And when you want to do another down
And cultivate advantage for yourself,
And when the wish to gossip comes to you,
It's then that like a log you should remain.

53. Impatience, indolence, faint heartedness,
And likewise haughty speech and insolence,
Attachment to your side—when these arise,
It's then that like a log you should remain.

54. Examine thus yourself from every side.
Note harmful thoughts and every futile striving.
Thus it is that heroes in the bodhisattva path
Apply the remedies to keep a steady mind.

55. With perfect and unyielding faith,
     With steadfastness, respect, and courtesy,
     With modesty and conscientiousness,
     Work calmly for the happiness of others.

56. Let us not be downcast by the warring wants
     Of childish persons quarreling.
     Their thoughts are bred from conflict and emotion.
     Let us understand and treat them lovingly.

57. When doing virtuous acts, beyond reproach,
     To help ourselves, or for the sake of others,
     Let us always bear in mind the thought
     That we are self-less, like an apparition.

58. This supreme treasure of a human life,
     So long awaited, now at last attained!
     Reflecting always thus, maintain your mind
     As steady as Sumeru, king of mountains.

59. When vultures with their love of flesh
     Are tugging at this body all around,
     Small will be the joy you get from it, O mind!
     Why *are* you so besotted with it now?

60. Why, O mind, do you protect this body,
     Claiming it as though it were yourself?
     You and it are each a separate entity,
     How ever can it be of use to you?

61. Why not cling, O foolish mind, to something clean,
     A figure carved in wood, or some such thing?
     Why do you protect and guard
     An unclean engine for the making of impurity?

62. First, with mind's imagination,
    Shed the covering of skin,
    And with the blade of wisdom, strip
    The flesh from off the bony frame.

63. And when you have divided all the bones,
    And searched right down amid the very marrow,
    You should look and ask the question:
    Where is "thingness" to be found?

64. If, persisting in the search,
    You find no underlying object,
    Why still cherish—and with such desire—
    The fleshly form you now possess?

65. Its filth you cannot eat, O mind;
    Its blood likewise is not for you to drink;
    Its innards, too, unsuitable to suck—
    This body, what then will you make of it?

66. As second best, it may indeed be kept
    As food to feed the vulture and the fox.
    The value of this human form
    Lies only in the way that it is used.

67. Whatever you may do to guard and keep it,
    What will you do when
    The Lord of Death, the ruthless, unrelenting,
    Steals and throws it to the birds and dogs?

68. Slaves unsuitable for work
    Are not rewarded with supplies and clothing.
    This body, though you pamper it, will leave you—
    Why exhaust yourself with such great labor?

69. So pay this body due remuneration,
    But then be sure to make it work for you.
    But do not lavish everything
    On what will not bring perfect benefit.

70. Regard your body as a vessel,
    A simple boat for going here and there.
    Make of it a wish-fulfilling gem
    To bring about the benefit of beings.

71. Thus with free, untrammeled mind,
    Put on an ever-smiling countenance.
    Rid yourself of scowling, wrathful frowns,
    And be a true and honest friend to all.

72. Do not, acting inconsiderately,
    Move furniture and chairs so noisily around.
    Likewise do not open doors with violence.
    Take pleasure in the practice of humility.

73. Herons, cats, and burglars
    Go silently and carefully;
    This is how they gain what they intend.
    And one who practices this path behaves likewise.

74. When useful admonitions come unasked
    To those with skill in counseling their fellows,
    Let them welcome them with humble gratitude,
    And always strive to learn from everyone.

75. Praise all who speak the truth,
    And say, "Your words are excellent."
    And when you notice others acting well,
    Encourage them in terms of warm approval.

76. Extol them even in their absence;
    When they're praised by others, do the same.
    But when the qualities they praise are yours,
    Appreciate their skill in knowing qualities.

77. The goal of every act is happiness itself,
    Though, even with great wealth, it's rarely found.
    So take your pleasure in the qualities of others.
    Let them be a heartfelt joy to you.

78. By acting thus, in this life you'll lose nothing;
    In future lives, great bliss will come to you.
    The sin of envy brings not joy but pain,
    And in the future, dreadful suffering.

79. Speak with honest words, coherently,
    With candor, in a clear, harmonious voice.
    Abandon partiality, rejection, and attraction,
    And speak with moderation, gently.

80. And catching sight of others, think
    That it will be through them
    That you will come to buddhahood.
    So look on them with open, loving hearts.

81. Always fired by highest aspiration,
    Laboring to implement the antidotes,[50]
    You will gather virtues in the fields
    Of qualities, of benefits, of sorrow.[51]

82. Acting thus with faith and understanding,
    You will always undertake good works.
    And in whatever actions you perform,
    You'll not be calculating, with your eye on others.

83.   The six perfections,[52] giving and the rest,
        Progress in sequence, growing in importance.
        The great should never be supplanted by the less,
        And it is others' good that is the highest goal.

84.   Therefore understand this well
        And always labor for the benefit of beings.
        The far-seeing masters of compassion
        Permit, to this end, that which is proscribed.[53]

85.   Eat only what is needful;
        Share with those who have embraced the discipline.
        To those, defenseless, fallen into evil states,
        Give all except the three robes of religion.

86.   The body, apt to practice sacred teaching,
        Should not be harmed in trivial pursuits.
        If this advice is kept, the wishes of all beings
        Will swiftly and completely be attained.

87.   They should not give up their bodies
        Whose compassion is not pure and perfect.
        But let them, in this world and those to come,
        Subject their bodies to the service of the supreme goal.

88.   Do not teach to those without respect,
        To those who like the sick wear cloths around their heads,
        To those who proudly carry weapons, staffs, or parasols,
        And those who keep their hats upon their heads.

89.   Do not teach the vast and deep[54] to those
        Upon the lower paths, nor, as a monk,
        To women unescorted. Teach with equal honor
        Low and high[55] according to their path.

90. Those suited to the teachings vast and deep,
    Should not be introduced to lesser paths.
    But basic practice you should not forsake,
    Confused by talk of sūtras and of mantras.[56]

91. Your spittle and your toothbrushes,
    When thrown away, should be concealed.
    And it is wrong to foul with urine
    Public thoroughfares and water springs.

92. When eating do not gobble noisily,
    Nor stuff and cram your gaping mouth.
    And do not sit with legs outstretched,
    Nor rudely rub your hands together.

93. Do not sit upon a horse, on beds or seats,
    With women of another house, alone.[57]
    All that you have seen, or have been told,
    To be offensive—this you should avoid.

94. Not rudely pointing with your finger,
    But rather with a reverent gesture showing,
    With the whole right hand outstretched—
    This is how to indicate the road.

95. Do not wave your arms with uncouth gestures.
    With gentle sounds and finger snaps[58]
    Express yourself with modesty—
    For acting otherwise is impolite excess.

96. Lie down to sleep with posture and direction
    Of the Buddha when he passed into nirvāṇa.
    And first, with clear resolve,
    Decide that you'll be swift to rise again.

97.　The bodhisattva's acts
　　　Are boundless, as the teachings say,
　　　And all these practices that cleanse the mind
　　　Embrace—until success has been attained.

98.　Reciting thrice, by day, by night,
　　　The Sūtra in Three Sections,⁵⁹
　　　Relying on the buddhas and the bodhisattvas,
　　　Purify the rest of your transgressions.

99.　And therefore in whatever time or place,
　　　For your own good and for the good of others,
　　　Be diligent to implement
　　　The teachings given for that situation.

100.　There is indeed no virtue
　　　That the buddhas' offspring should not learn.
　　　To one with mastery therein,
　　　There is no action destitute of merit.

101.　Directly, then, or indirectly,
　　　All you do must be for others' sake.
　　　And solely for their welfare dedicate
　　　Your actions for the gaining of enlightenment.

102.　Never, at the cost of life or limb,
　　　Forsake your virtuous friend, your teacher,
　　　Learned in the meaning of the Mahāyāna,⁶⁰
　　　Supreme in practice of the bodhisattva path.

103.　For thus you must depend upon your guru,
　　　As you will find described in Shrī Sambhava's life,⁶¹
　　　And elsewhere in the teachings of the Buddha:
　　　These be sure to study, reading in the sūtras.

104. The training you will find described
     Within the sūtras. Therefore read and study them.
     The Sūtra of the Essence of the Sky[62]—
     This is the text that should be studied first.

105. The *Digest of All Disciplines*
     Contains a detailed and extensive explanation
     Of all that must be practiced come what may.
     So this is something you should read repeatedly.

106. From time to time, for sake of brevity,
     Consult the *Digest of the Sūtras*.[63]
     And those two works peruse with diligence
     That noble Nāgārjuna has composed.

107. Whatever in these works is not proscribed
     Be sure to undertake and implement.
     And what you see there, perfectly fulfill,
     And so safeguard the minds of worldly beings.

108. To keep a guard again and yet again
     Upon the state and actions of our thoughts and deeds—
     This and only this defines
     The nature and the sense of mental watchfulness.

109. But all this must be acted out in truth,
     For what is to be gained by mouthing syllables?
     What invalid was ever helped
     By merely reading in the doctor's treatises?

Patience

1.   Good works gathered in a thousand ages,
    Such as deeds of generosity,
    Or offerings to the blissful ones—
    A single flash of anger shatters them.

2.   No evil is there similar to anger,
    No austerity to be compared with patience.
    Steep yourself, therefore, in patience—
    In all ways, urgently, with zeal.

3.   Those tormented by the pain of anger
    Will never know tranquillity of mind—
    Strangers they will be to every pleasure;
    Sleep departs them, they can never rest.

4.   Noble chieftains full of hate
    Will be attacked and slain
    By even those who look to them
    For honors and possessions.

5.   From family and friends estranged,
    And shunned by those attracted by their bounty,
    Men of anger have no joy,
    Forsaken by all happiness and peace.

6.   All these ills are brought about by wrath,
Our sorrow-bearing enemy.
But those who seize and crush their anger down
Will find their joy in this and future lives.

7.   Getting what I do not want,
And all that hinders my desire—
There my mind finds fuel for misery;
Anger springs from it, oppressing me.

8.   Therefore I will utterly destroy
The sustenance of this my enemy,
My foe, whose sole intention is
To bring me injury and sorrow.

9.   So come what may, I'll never harm
My cheerful happiness of mind.
Depression never brings me what I want;
My virtue will be warped and marred by it.

10.   If there is a remedy when trouble strikes,
What reason is there for despondency?
And if there is no help for it,
What use is there in being sad?

11.   Pain, humiliation, insults, or rebukes—
We do not want them
Either for ourselves or those we love.
For those we do not like, it's quite the opposite!

12.   The cause of happiness comes rarely,
And many are the seeds of suffering!
But if I have no pain, I'll never long for freedom;
Therefore, O my mind, be steadfast!

13.   The Karna folk, devoted to the Goddess,[64]
      Endure the meaningless austerities
      Of being cut and burned.
      Why am I so timid on the path of freedom?

14.   There's nothing that does not grow light
      Through habit and familiarity.
      Putting up with little cares
      I'll train myself to bear with great adversity.

15.   And do I not already bear with common irritations—
      Bites and stings of snakes and flies,
      Experiences of hunger and of thirst,
      And painful rashes on my skin?

16.   Heat and cold, the wind and rain,
      Sickness, prison, beatings—
      I'll not fret about such things.
      To do so only aggravates my trouble.

17.   There are some whose bravery increases
      At the sight of their own blood,
      While some lose all their strength and faint
      When it's another's blood they see!

18.   This results from how the mind is set,
      In steadfastness or cowardice.
      And so I'll scorn all injury,
      And hardships I will disregard!

19.   When sorrows fall upon the wise,
      Their minds remain serene and undisturbed.
      For in their war against defiled emotion,
      Many are the hardships, as in every battle.

20.   Thinking scorn of every pain,
    And vanquishing such foes as hatred:
    These are exploits of a conquering hero.
    The rest is slaying what is dead already!

21.   Suffering also has its worth.
    Through sorrow, pride is driven out
    And pity felt for those who wander in saṃsāra;
    Evil is avoided, goodness seems delightful.

22.   I am not angry with my bile and other humors—
    Fertile source of pain and suffering!
    So why should I resent my fellow creatures,
    Victims, too, of like conditions?[65]

23.   For though they are unlooked for, undesired,
    These ills afflict us all the same.
    And likewise, though unwanted and unsought,
    Defilements nonetheless are quick to come.

24.   Never thinking, "Now I will be angry,"
    People are impulsively caught up in anger.
    Irritation, likewise, comes—
    Though never plans to be experienced!

25.   Every injury whatever,
    The whole variety of evil deeds
    Is brought about by circumstances.
    None is independent, none autonomous.

26.   Conditions, once assembled, have no thought
    That now they will give rise to some result.
    And that which is engendered does not think
    That it has been produced by such conditions.

27. That which is referred to as the Primal Substance,
     That which has been labeled as the Self
     Do not come into being thinking
     "That is how I will arise."

28. That which is not manifest is not yet there,
     So what could want to come to be?
     And permanently drawn toward its object,
     It can never cease from being so.[66]

29. Indeed! This Self, if permanent,
     Is certainly impassible like space itself.
     And should it meet with other factors,
     How should they affect it, since it is unchanging?

30. If, when things occur, it stays unchanged and as before,
     What influence has action had on it?
     They say that this affects the Self,
     But what connection could there be between them?[67]

31. All things, then, depend on something else;
     On this depends the fact that none are independent.
     Knowing this, we will not be annoyed at objects
     That resemble magical appearances.

32. "Resistance," you may say, "is out of place,
     For what will be opposed by whom?"
     The stream of suffering is cut through by patience;
     There's nothing inappropriate in wanting that!

33. Thus, when enemies or friends
     Are seen to act improperly,
     Be calm and call to mind
     That everything arises from conditions.

34. If things occurred to living beings
    Following their wishes and intentions,
    How could sorrow ever come to them—
    For there is no one who desires to suffer?

35. Yet carelessly, all unaware,
    They tear themselves on thorns and briars;
    And ardent in pursuit of wives and goods,
    They starve themselves of nourishment.

36. Some hang themselves or leap into the void,
    Or eat bad food or swallow deadly poison,
    Or by their evil conduct
    Bring destruction on themselves.

37. For when affliction seizes them,
    They kill themselves, the selves they love so much.
    So how could they not be the cause
    Of pain and suffering for others?

38. And when, as victims of defilement,
    Beings even cause their own destruction,
    Even if compassion does not rise in us,
    We can at least refrain from being angry.

39. If those who are like wanton children
    Are by nature prone to injure others,
    What point is there in being angry—
    Like resenting fire for its heat?

40. And if their faults are fleeting and contingent,
    If living beings are by nature wholesome,
    It's likewise senseless to resent them—
    As well be angry at the sky for having clouds!

41. Although indeed it is the stick that hurts me,
     I am angry at the one who wields it, striking me.
     But he is driven and impelled by anger—
     So it is his wrath I should resent.

42. I it was who in the past
     Did harm to beings such as these.
     And so, when others do me mischief,
     It is only just that they should injure me.

43. Their weapons and my body—
     Both are causes of my suffering!
     They their weapons drew, while I held out my body.
     Who then is more worthy of my anger?

44. This human form is like a running sore;
     Merely touched, it cannot stand the pain!
     I'm the one who clings to it with blind attachment;
     Whom should I resent when pain occurs?

45. We who are like senseless children
     Shrink from suffering, but love its causes.
     We hurt ourselves; our pain is self-inflicted!
     Why should *others* be the object of our anger?

46. Who indeed should I be angry with?
     This pain is all my own contriving—
     Likewise all the janitors of hell
     And all the groves of razor trees!⁶⁸

47. Those who harm me come against me,
     Summoned by my evil karma.
     But they will be the ones who go to hell,
     And so it is myself who bring *their* ruin.

48. Because of them, and through the exercise of patience,
    My many sins are cleansed and purified.
    But they will be the ones who, thanks to me,
    Will have the long-drawn agonies of hell.

49. Therefore I am *their* tormentor!
    Therefore it is they who bring me benefit!
    Thus with what perversity, pernicious mind,
    Will you be angry with your enemies?

50. For if a patient quality of mind
    Is mine, I shall avoid the pains of hell.
    But though indeed I save myself,
    What of my foes, what fate's in store for them?

51. If I repay them harm for harm,
    Indeed they'll not be saved thereby;
    And all my noble actions will be spoiled,
    Austerity of patience brought to nothing.

52. The mind is bodiless:
    By no one can it be destroyed.
    And yet it grasps the body tightly,
    Falling victim to the body's pain.

53. Scorn and hostile words,
    And comments that I do not like to hear—
    My body is not harmed by them.
    What reason do you have, O mind, for your resentment?

54. Contempt and scorn that others show me
    Now and in my future lives—
    Since none of it can bite and swallow me,
    Why is it that I'm so averse to it?

55.   Perhaps I turn from it because
      It hinders me from having what I want.
      But all my property I'll leave behind,
      While sins will keep me steady company.

56.   Better far for me to die today,
      Than live a long and evil life.
      However great may be my length of days,
      The pain of dying will be all the same.

57.   One man dreams he lives a hundred years
      Of happiness, but then he wakes.
      Another dreams an instant's joy,
      But then he, likewise, wakes.

58.   And when they wake, the happiness of both
      Is finished, never to return.
      Likewise, when the hour of death comes round,
      Our lives are over, whether brief or long.

59.   Though we be rich in worldly goods,
      Delighting in our wealth for many years,
      Despoiled and stripped as though by thieves,
      We must go naked and with empty hands.

60.   Perhaps we'll claim that by our wealth we live,
      And living, gather merit, dissipating evil.
      But if we're ruthless for the sake of gain,
      It's evil we will gather, dissipating merit!

61.   What use then will our lives have been
      When all is so degenerate and spoiled?
      What use is there in living such a life
      When evil is the only consequence?

62.   If, when others slander us, we claim
       Our anger is because they harm themselves,
       How is it we do not resent
       Their slander when it's aimed at someone else?

63.   If we bear with such antipathy,
       Remarking that it's due to other factors,
       Why are we impatient when they slander us?
       Emotion, after all, has been the cause of it.

64.   Even those who vilify and undermine
       The sacred Doctrine, images, and stūpas
       Are not the proper objects of our anger;
       The buddhas are themselves untouched thereby.

65.   And even if our teachers, relatives, and friends
       Are now the object of aggression,
       All derives from factors just explained.
       This we should perceive, and curb our wrath.

66.   Beings suffer injury alike
       From lifeless things as well as living beings;
       So why be angry only with the latter?
       Rather let us simply bear with harm.

67.   Some do evil things because of ignorance,
       Some respond with anger, being ignorant.
       Which of them is faultless in his acts?
       To whom shall error be attributed?

68.   Rather, why did I do evil in the past,
       That cause me harm at others' hands?
       All that happens is the fruit of karma;
       Why then should I now be angry?

69. This I see and therefore, come what may,
    I'll hold fast to the virtuous path
    And foster in the hearts of all
    An attitude of mutual love.

70. For when a building is ablaze
    And flames leap out from house to house,
    The wise course is to take and fling away
    The straw and anything that spreads the fire.

71. In fear that merit might be all consumed,
    We should at once cast far away
    Our mind's attachments:
    Tinder for the fiery flames of hate.

72. Is not a man relieved when, though condemned to death,
    He's freed, his hand cut off in ransom for his life?
    Enduring likewise merely human ills,
    Am I not happy to avoid the pains of hell?

73. If pains of even this, my present life,
    Are now beyond my strength to bear,
    Why do I not overthrow my anger,
    Cause of future sorrows in infernal torment?

74. For sake of gaining all that I desired,
    A thousand times I underwent
    The tortures of the realms of hell—
    Achieving nothing for myself and others.

75. The present aches are nothing to compare with those,
    And yet great benefits may come from them.
    These troubles that dispel the pains of wanderers—
    How could I not rejoice in them?

76.   When others take delight
       In giving praise to those endowed with talents,
       Why, O mind, do you not find
       A joy, likewise, in praising them?

77.   The pleasure that you gain therefrom
       Itself gives rise to stainless happiness.
       It's urged on us by all the holy ones,
       And is the perfect way of winning others.

78.   "But they're the ones who'll have the happiness," you say.
       If this then is a joy you would resent,
       Abandon paying wages and returning favors:
       You will be the loser—both in this life and the next![69]

79.   When praise is heaped upon your merits,
       You're keen that others should rejoice in them.
       But when the compliment is paid to others,
       Your joy is oh so slow and grudging.

80.   You who want the happiness of beings,
       Have wished to be enlightened for their sake.
       So why should others irk you when
       They find some little pleasure for themselves?

81.   If you truly wish that beings be enlightened,
       Venerated by the triple world,
       When petty marks of favor come their way,
       Why, oh why, are you in torment?

82.   When dependents who rely on you,
       To whom you are obliged to give support,
       Find for themselves the means of livelihood,
       Will you not be happy, will you once again be angry?

83. If even this you do not want for beings,
     How could you want buddhahood for them?
     And how can anyone have bodhichitta
     And resent the good that others have?

84. If someone else receives a gift,
     Or if that gift stays in the benefactor's house,
     In neither case will it be yours—
     So, given or withheld, why is it your concern?

85. Tell me, why don't you resent yourself,
     You who throw your merit, faith,
     And all your qualities so far away?
     Why do you not cultivate the cause of riches?

86. All the evil you have done
     You cheerfully neglect to purify.
     And do you further wish to match yourself
     With others who have earned their merit?

87. If unhappiness befalls your enemy,
     Why should this be a cause for your rejoicing?
     The wishes of your mind alone,
     Will not in fact contrive his injury.

88. And if your hostile wishes *were* to bring them harm,
     Again, what cause of joy is that to you?
     "Why, then I should be satisfied!"—are these your thoughts?
     Is anything more ruinous than that?

89. Caught upon the hook, unbearable and sharp,
     Cast by the fisherman, my own defilements,
     I'll be flung into the cauldrons of the pit,
     And surely parboiled by the janitors of hell!

90. The rigmarole of praise and fame
    Serves not to increase merit or one's span of life,
    Bestowing neither health nor strength
    And nothing for the body's ease.

91. If I am wise in what is good for me,
    I'll ask what benefit these bring.
    For if it's entertainment I desire,
    I might as well resort to alcohol and cards![70]

92. We lose our lives, our wealth we squander,
    All for reputation's sake.
    What use are words, and whom will they delight
    When we are dead and in our graves?

93. Children can't help crying when
    Their sand castles come crumbling down.
    Our minds are so like them
    When praise and reputation start to fail.

94. Short-lived sound, devoid of intellect,
    Can never in itself intend to praise us.
    "But it's the joy that others take in me," you say—
    Are these the shoddy causes of your pleasure?

95. What is it to me if others should delight
    In someone else, or even in myself?
    Their pleasure's theirs, and theirs alone.
    What part of it could be for my enjoyment?

96. If I am happy at the joy of those who take delight,
    Then everyone should be a source of joy to me.
    Why, when glory goes elsewhere,
    Am I not happy with this cause of happiness?[71]

97. The satisfaction that is mine
     From thinking "I am being praised,"
     Is unacceptable to common sense,
     And nothing but the silly ways of children.

98. Praise and compliments disturb me,
     Sapping my revulsion with saṃsāra.
     I start to covet others' qualities,
     And thus all excellence degenerates.

99. Those who stay close by me, then,
     To ruin my good name and cut me down to size
     Are surely there protecting me
     From falling into ruin in the realms of sorrow.

100. For I am one who strives for freedom—
     I must not be caught by wealth and honors.
     How could I be angry with the ones
     Who work to loose me from my fetters?

101. They, like Buddha's very blessing,
     Bar my way, determined as I am
     To plunge myself headlong in sorrow:
     How could I be angry with them?

102. We should not be angry, saying,
     "They are obstacles to virtue."
     Is not patience the supreme austerity,
     And is this not my chosen discipline?

103. If I fail to practice patience,
     Hindered by my own deficiency,
     I am myself the obstacle to gaining
     Merit, yet so close at hand.

104. For nothing comes except through other factors,
     And comes to be, those factors being present.
     If one thing is the cause of something else,
     How could it then be said to hinder it?

105. The beggars who arrive at proper times
     Are not an obstacle to generosity.
     We cannot say that those who give the vows
     Are causing hindrances to ordination!

106. The beggars in this world are many,
     Attackers are comparatively few.
     For as I do no harm to others,
     Those who do me injury are rare.

107. So like a treasure found at home,
     Enriching me without fatigue,
     All enemies are helpers in my bodhisattva work
     And therefore they should be a joy to me.

108. The fruits of patience are for them and me,
     For both of us have brought it into being.
     And yet to them they must be offered first,
     For of my patience they have been the cause.

109. Yet if I say my foe should not be praised
     Since he did not intend to stimulate my patience,
     Why do I revere the sacred Doctrine,
     Cause indeed of my attainment?

110. "This enemy conspired to harm me," I protest,
     "And therefore should receive no honors."
     But had he worked to help me, like a doctor,
     How could I have brought forth patience?

111. Because of those whose minds are full of anger,
     I engender patience in myself.
     They are thus the cause of patience,
     Fit for veneration, like the Doctrine.

112. The worlds of beings are a buddhafield,[72]
     Thus the Mighty Lord has taught.
     For many who have sought the happiness of others
     Have gone beyond, attaining to perfection.

113. Thus the state of buddhahood depends
     On beings and the buddhas equally.
     By what tradition is it then
     That buddhas, but not beings, are revered?

114. Their aims are not, of course, the same,
     But it is by their fruits that we should know them.
     And so we see the excellence of beings—
     Beings and the buddhas are indeed the same!

115. Offerings made to one who loves
     Reveals the eminence of living beings.[73]
     Merit that accrues from faith in Buddha
     Reveals in turn the Buddha's eminence.

116. Since they are both the means of winning buddhahood,
     We say that beings are the same as buddhas,
     Even though they are not equal
     In the boundless ocean of a buddha's merits.

117. Yet if a tiny part of that great merit
     Were found to be contained in certain beings' hearts,
     The three worlds made in offering to them
     Would be a slight, a very little thing.

118. A share in bringing forth the supreme state of buddhahood
      Is thus possessed by everyone.
      This demonstrates the reason why
      They are the proper object of my reverence.

119. As buddhas are my constant friends,
      Boundless in the benefits they bring to me,
      How else may I repay their goodness,
      But by making living beings happy?

120. By helping beings we repay the ones
      Who gave themselves for us and plunged into the hells.
      Should beings therefore do great harm to me,
      I'll strive to bring them only benefit.

121. For if the ones who are my lords and teachers,
      For beings' sake are careless even of their bodies,
      Why should I, a fool, behave with such conceit?
      Why should I not become the slave of others?

122. Buddhas are made happy by the joy of beings;
      They sorrow, they lament when beings suffer.
      Bringing joy to beings, then, I please the buddhas also—
      Offending them, the buddhas I offend.

123. Just as when a man who's tortured in a fire,
      Remains unmoved by little favors done to him,
      There's no way to delight the great compassionate buddhas,
      While we ourselves are causes of another's pain.

124. The damage I have done to wandering beings
      Saddens all the buddhas in their great compassion.
      Therefore, all these sins I will confess today
      And pray that they will bear with me.

125. And that I might rejoice the buddhas' hearts,
      I will be master of myself, and be the servant of the world—
      And not respond though others trample, wound, or kill me.
      Now let the guardians of the world rejoice!

126. The great compassionate lords consider as their own[74]
      All wanderers—of this there is no doubt.
      Beings, then, are Buddha's very self.
      Thus how can I not treat them with respect?

127. Venerating them will please the buddhas' hearts,
      And perfectly secure the welfare of myself.
      This will drive away the sorrows of the world,
      And therefore it will be my constant practice.

128. Imagine that the steward of a king
      Does injury to multitudes of people.
      Those among the injured who are wise
      Will not respond with violence, even if they can.

129. For stewards, after all, are not alone.
      They are supported by the kingly power.
      Likewise I should not make light
      Of lesser men who do me little injuries.

130. For they have guardians of hell for allies
      And also the compassionate buddhas.
      Therefore I'll respect all living beings,
      As though they were the subjects of that wrathful king.

131. And yet, the pains of hell to be endured
      Through making living beings suffer—
      Could these ever be unleashed on us
      By all the fury of an angry king?

132. And even if that king were pleased,
     Enlightenment he could not give to us,
     For this will only be achieved
     By bringing happiness to living beings.

133. Granted, then, that future buddhahood
     Is forged through bringing happiness to beings;
     How can I not see that glory, fame, and pleasure
     Even in this life will likewise come?

134. For patience in saṃsāra brings such things
     As beauty, health, and good renown.
     Its fruit is great longevity,
     The vast contentment of a universal king.

Heroic Perseverance

1. Thus with patience I will bravely persevere.[75]
    Through zeal it is that I shall reach enlightenment.
    If no wind blows, then nothing stirs,
    And neither is there merit without perseverance.

2. Heroic perseverance means delight in virtue.
    Its contrary may be defined as laziness:
    An inclination for unwholesome ways,
    Despondency, and self-contempt.

3. Complacent pleasure in the joys of idleness,
    A craving for repose and sleep,
    No qualms about the sorrows of saṃsāra:
    These are the source and nurse of laziness.

4. Snared by the trapper of defiled emotion,
    Enmeshed and taken in the toils of birth,
    How could I not know that thus I've strayed
    Into the mouth, the very jaws, of Death?

5. Don't you see how one by one
    Death comes to claim your fellow men?
    And yet you slumber on so soundly,
    Like a buffalo beside its butcher.

6.   All paths of flight are blocked,
The Lord of Death now has you in his sights.
How can you take pleasure in your food?
How can you delight to rest and sleep?

7.   Death will be so quick to swoop on you;
Gather merit till that moment comes!
Wait till then to banish laziness?
Then there'll be no time, what will you do?

8.   "This I have not done. And this I'm only starting.
And this—I'm only halfway through. . . . "
Then is the sudden coming of the Lord of Death,
And oh, the thought "Alas, I'm finished!"

9.   Your tear-stained cheeks, your red and swollen eyes,
Such will be the depths of your distress.
You'll gaze into the faces of your hopeless friends,
And see the coming servants of the Deadly Lord.

10.   The memory of former sins will torture you;
The screams and din of hell break on your ears.
With very terror you will foul yourself;
What will you do then, in such extremity of fear?

11.   And if you are so scared while still alive,
Like fishes writhing on the open ground,
What need to speak of pain unbearable
In hells created by past evil deeds?

12.   The hells in which the boiling molten bronze
Will burn your body, tender like a baby's flesh—
All is now prepared, your former deeds have done it!
How can you lie back, so free of care?

13.　Much harm will come to those with small forbearance,
　　　Who wish to have the fruit without endeavor.
　　　Seized by death, they'll cry out like the gods:[76]
　　　"Alas I fall, by pain and sorrow crushed."

14.　Take advantage of this human boat;
　　　Free yourself from sorrow's mighty stream!
　　　This vessel will be later hard to find.
　　　The time that you have now, you fool, is not for sleep!

15.　You turn your back upon the sacred Doctrine,
　　　The supreme joy and boundless source of bliss.
　　　What pleasure can you have in mere amusement
　　　Straying to the causes of your misery?

16.　Do not be downcast, but marshal all your strength;
　　　Take heart and be the master of yourself!
　　　Practice the equality of self and other;
　　　Practice the exchange of self and other.[77]

17.　"Oh, but how could *I* become enlightened?"
　　　Don't excuse yourself with such despondency!
　　　The buddhas, who declare the truth,
　　　Have spoken and indeed proclaimed,

18.　That if they bring forth strength of perseverance,
　　　The very bees and flies and stinging gnats
　　　Or grubs will find with ease
　　　Enlightenment so hard to find!

19.　Able to distinguish good from ill,
　　　If I, by birth and lineage of human kind,
　　　Devote myself to bodhisattva training,
　　　Why should I not gain the state of buddhahood?

20. "That I must give away my life and limbs
    Alarms and frightens me"—if so you say,
    Your terror is misplaced. Confused,
    You fail to see what's hard and what is easy.

21. For myriads of ages, measureless, uncounted,
    Your body has been cut, impaled,
    Burned, flayed—for times past numbering!
    Yet none of this has brought you buddhahood.

22. The hardships suffered on the path to buddhahood
    Are different, for their span is limited,
    And likened to the pain of an incision
    Made to cure the harm of hidden ailments.

23. The doctors and those skilled in healing arts,
    Use bitter remedies to cure our ills.
    Likewise we, to uproot dreadful sorrow,
    Should bear what are indeed but little pains.

24. And yet the Supreme Healer does not use,
    Like them, these common remedies.
    With antidotes of extreme tenderness
    He soothes away intense and boundless suffering.

25. Our guide instructs us to begin
    By giving food or other little charities,
    That later, step by step, the habit once acquired,
    We may be able to donate our very flesh.

26. For when one has the view that sees
    Equality between one's body and the food one gives,
    Why then! What hardship can there be
    In giving up, relinquishing, one's very flesh?

27. Sin has been abandoned, thus there is no pain.
    Mind is skilled, and thus there is no sorrow.
    For so it is that mind and body both
    Are injured by false views and sinfulness.

28. Merit is the true cause of the body's ease,
    While happiness of mind is brought about by training.
    What can sadden those who have compassion,
    Who linger in saṃsāra for the sake of beings?

29. For through their power of bodhichitta,
    Former sins are totally consumed,
    And merit, ocean-vast, is gathered in;
    Therefore we say they're higher than the shrāvakas.[78]

30. For, mounted on the horse of bodhichitta,
    That puts to flight all mournful weariness,
    Who could ever be dejected,
    Riding such a steed from joy to joy?

31. The forces that secure the good of beings
    Are aspiration, firmness, joy, and moderation.
    Aspiration grows through fear of suffering
    And contemplation of the benefits to be attained.

32. Therefore leaving everything that is adverse to it,
    I'll labor to increase my perseverance—
    Through cheerful effort, keenness, self-control,
    Through aspiration, firmness, joy, and moderation.

33. Thus the boundless evils of myself and others—
    I alone must bring them all to nothing,
    Even though a single of these ills
    May take unnumbered ages to exhaust!

34.   And yet for this great enterprise I do not see
      Within myself the slightest aptitude—
      I whose destiny is boundless suffering,
      Why does not my heart now burst asunder?[79]

35.   All virtues for my own and others' sake,
      Though they be many, I must now accomplish,
      Even if for each I must
      Endeavor for unnumbered ages.

36.   Acquaintance I have never gained
      With even part of such great qualities.
      So strange to waste in trivial pursuits
      This life that chance has brought to me!

37.   Offerings to the buddhas I have never made;
      No feasts were ever held through my donations;
      No works have I accomplished for the Teachings;
      The wishes of the poor, alas, I left unsatisfied.

38.   The frightened I have not encouraged,
      And to the weary I have given no rest.
      My mother's birth pangs and her womb's discomfort,
      These alone are my accomplishments!

39.   Thus my poverty, my lack of fortune,
      Come from failure to aspire to Dharma
      In the past and likewise in the present!
      Whoever would reject this aspiration?

40.   Aspiration is the root of every virtue,
      Thus the Mighty One has said.
      And aspiration's root in turn
      Is constant meditation on the fruits of action.

41. The body's pains, anxieties of mind,
    Our every fear and trepidation,
    Separation from the objects of our wanting:
    Such is the harvest of our sinful deeds.

42. If my acts are wholesome, mirroring my mind,
    Then no matter where I turn my steps,
    Respect and honor will be paid to me,
    The fruit and recompense of merit.

43. But if, in search of happiness, my works are evil,
    Then no matter where I turn my steps,
    The knives of misery will cut me down—
    The wage and retribution of a sinful life.

44. I will arise, through virtue, in the cool heart of a fragrant, spreading
    lotus,
    Its petals opened in the Buddha's light,
    With glory nourished by the sweet words of the Conqueror,
    And live, the buddhas' heir, within the presence of Victorious
    Ones.[80]

45. Or else as wages for my sins, I'll be struck down, my skin flayed off
    by creatures
    Of the Lord of Death, who on my body pour the liquid bronze
    that's melted in the dreadful blaze.
    And pierced by burning swords and knives, my flesh
    Dismembered in a hundred parts, will fall upon the white-hot iron
    ground.

46. And so I will aspire and tend to virtue,
    And steep myself in it with great devotion.
    And with the method stated in the *Vajradhvaja*,[81]
    I will train in confident assurance.

47.   Let me first consider my resources—
      To start or not to start accordingly.
      For it is better not to start at all,
      Than to begin and then retrace my steps.

48.   For, acting thus, the pattern will return
      In later lives, and sin and pain will grow.
      And other actions will be left undone
      Or else will bear a meager fruit.

49.   Action, the afflictions, and ability:
      Three things to which my pride should be applied.[82]
      "I will do this, I myself, alone!"
      These words define my pride of action.

50.   Enfeebled by their minds' afflictions,
      Worldly folk are helpless to secure their happiness.
      Compared to those who wander, I am able—
      This indeed shall be my chosen task.

51.   When others give themselves to base activities,
      How can I connive as their companion?
      But I shall not refrain through pride or arrogance;
      My best way is to give up such conceit.

52.   When they find a dying serpent,
      Even crows behave like soaring eagles.
      Therefore if I'm weak and feeble-hearted,
      Even little faults will strike and injure me.[83]

53.   How will those who basely flee the conflict,
      Ever free themselves from their debility?
      But those who stand their ground with proud resolve
      Are hard to vanquish even by the mighty.

54. Therefore with a steadfast heart
    I'll get the better of my weaknesses.
    But if my failings get the upper hand,
    My wish to overcome the world is laughable indeed.

55. "I *will* be the victor over all;
    Nothing shall prevail and bring me down!"
    The lion-offspring of the Conqueror
    Should constantly abide in this proud confidence.[84]

56. Those whom arrogance and pride destroy
    Are thus defiled; they lack proud confidence.
    They fall into the power of an evil pride,
    But those with true pride will escape the enemy.

57. When arrogance inflates the mind,
    It draws it down to states of misery,
    Or else it ruins human birth, should this be gained.
    Thus one is born a slave, dependent for one's food—

58. Or feebleminded, ugly, without strength,
    The butt and laughingstock of everyone.
    Hapless creatures puffed up with conceit!
    If these you call the proud, then tell me who are wretched?

59. Those who uphold pride to vanquish pride, the enemy,
    Are truly proud, the victors in the war.
    Those who overwhelm the progress of that evil pride,
    Perfect the fruit of buddhahood and satisfy the longings of the
        world.

60. When you are beleaguered by defilements,
    Fight them in a thousand ways.
    Do not surrender to the host of the afflictions;
    Be like a lion in a crowd of foxes.

61. However great may be their peril,
    People will by reflex guard their eyes.
    And likewise I, regardless of all hardship,
    Must not fall beneath defilement's power.

62. Even though I may be burned to death,
    And though I may be killed, my head cut off,
    At no time will I bow and scrape
    Before that foe of mine, defiled emotion.[85]

62a. Thus in every time and place
    I will not wander from the wholesome path.

63. Like those who take great pleasure in their games,
    The bodhisattvas in their every deed
    Will feel the greatest joy, exhilaration,
    Pleasure that will never fade or pass.

64. People labor hard to gain contentment
    Though success is very far from sure;
    But how can they be happy if they do not labor,
    Those whose joy is in the work itself?

65. And since I never have enough of pleasure,
    Honey on the razor's edge,
    How could I have enough of merit,
    Fruits of which are happiness and peace?

66. The elephant, tormented by the noonday sun,
    Will dive into the waters of a lake,
    And likewise I must plunge into this work
    That I might bring it to completion.

67. If impaired by weakness or fatigue,
    I'll lay the work aside, the better to resume.
    And I will leave tasks completed,
    Anticipating thus the work to come.

68. As seasoned fighters face the swords
     Of enemies upon the battle line,
     Lightly dodge the weapons of defilement,
     And overcome the foe with nimble skill!

69. If, in the fray, the soldier drops his sword,
     In fright, he swiftly takes it up again.
     So likewise, if the arm of mindfulness is lost,
     In fear of hell be quick to get it back.

70. Just as seeping venom fills the body,
     Carried on the current of the blood,
     An evil thought that finds its chance,
     Will spread and permeate the mind.

71. Be like a frightened man, a brimming oil jar in his hand,
     And menaced by a swordsman saying:
     "Spill one drop and you shall die!"
     This is how the disciplined should hold themselves.

72. As such a man would leap in fright
     To find a snake coiled in his lap,
     If sleep and sluggishness beset me,
     I will instantly dispel them.

73. Every time, then, that I fail,
     I will reprove and vilify myself,
     Thinking long that by whatever means
     Such faults in future shall no more occur.

74. At all times and in any situation,
     Mindfulness will be my constant habit.
     This will be the cause whereby I aim
     To meet with teachers and fulfill the proper tasks.

75. By all means, then, before I start this work,
    That I might have the strength sufficient to the task,
    I will reflect upon these words on mindfulness
    And lightly rise to what is to be done.

76. The lichen hanging in the trees wafts to and fro,
    Stirred by every breath of wind;
    Likewise, all I do will be achieved,
    Enlivened by the movements of a joyful heart.

Meditation

1.   After cultivating diligence,
        Set your mind to concentrate.
        For those whose minds are slack and wandering
        Are caught between the fangs of the afflictions.

2.   In solitude, the mind and body
        Are not troubled by distraction.
        Therefore, leave this worldly life
        And totally abandon mental wandering.

3.   Because of loved ones and desire for gain,
        Disgust with worldly life does not arise.
        These, then, are the first things to renounce.
        Such are the reflections of a prudent man.

4.   Penetrative insight joined with calm abiding
        Utterly eradicates afflicted states.
        Knowing this, first search for calm abiding,
        Found by those who joyfully renounce the world.

5.   Beings, brief, ephemeral,
        Who fiercely cling to what is also passing,
        Will catch no glimpse of happiness
        For many thousands of their future lives.

6. And thus their minds will have no joy
    And therefore will not rest in equanimity.
    But even if they taste it, they are not content—
    And as before, the pain of longing stays.

7. If I long and crave for other beings,
    A veil is cast upon the perfect truth.
    Wholesome disillusion[86] melts away,
    And finally there comes the sting of pain.

8. My thoughts are all for them . . .
    And by degrees my life is frittered by.
    My family and friends all fade and pass, for whom
    The Doctrine is destroyed that leads to indestructibility.

9. For if I act like those who are like children,
    Sure it is that I shall fall to lower states.
    So why keep company with infants
    And go with them in ways so far from virtue?

10. One moment friends,
    The next, they're bitter enemies.
    Even pleasant things arouse their discontent:
    Worldly people—hard it is to please them!

11. A beneficial word and they resent it,
    While all they do is turn me from the good.
    And if to what they say I close my ears,
    Their anger burns, the cause of lower states.

12. Jealous of superiors, they vie with equals,
    Proud to those below, they strut when praised.
    Say something untoward, they seethe with rage:
    What good was ever had from childish folk?

13. Keep company with them and what will follow?
    Self-aggrandizement and scorn for others,
    Talk about the "good things" of saṃsāra—
    Every kind of vice is sure to come.

14. Only ruin can result
    From links like these, between yourself and others.
    For they will bring no benefit to you,
    And you in turn can bring them nothing good.

15. Therefore flee the company of childish people.
    Greet them, when you meet, with smiles
    That keep on terms of pleasant courtesy,
    While not inviting close familiarity.

16. Like bees that get their honey from the flowers,
    Take only what is consonant with Dharma.
    Treat them like first-time acquaintances,
    Without encouraging a close relationship.

17. "Oh, I am rich, surrounded by attention,
    I have so much, and life is wonderful!"
    Nourish such complacency and later,
    After death, your fears will start!

18. Indeed, O foolish and afflicted mind,
    You want, you crave for everything,
    This "everything" will grow and turn
    To suffering increased a thousandfold.

19. Since this is so, the wise man does not crave,
    For from such craving fear and anguish come.
    And fix this firmly in your understanding:
    All that may be wished for will by nature fade to nothing.

20. For people may have gained a wealth of riches,
    Enjoying reputation, sweet renown.
    But who can say where they have gone to now,
    With all the baggage of their gold and fame?

21. Why should I be pleased when people praise me?
    Others there will be who scorn and criticize.
    And why despondent when I'm blamed,
    Since there'll be others who think well of me?

22. So many are the wants and tendencies of beings,
    Even Buddha could not please them all—
    Of such an evil man as me no need to speak!
    Better to give up such worldly thoughts.

23. People scorn the poor who have no wealth,
    They also criticize the rich who have it.
    What pleasure can derive from keeping company
    With people such as these, so difficult to please?

24. Unless they have their way in everything,
    These children are bereft of happiness.
    And so, shun friendship with the childish,
    Thus the Tathāgata has declared.

25. In woodlands, haunt of stag and bird,
    Among the trees where no dissension jars,
    It's there I would keep pleasant company!
    When might I be off to make my dwelling there?

26. When shall I depart to make my home
    In cave or empty shrine or under spreading tree,
    With, in my breast, a free, unfettered heart,
    Which never turns to cast a backward glance?

27.   When might I abide in such a place,
    A place unclaimed, by nature ownerless,
    That's wide and unconfined, a place where I might stay
    At liberty without attachment?

28.   When might I be free of fear,
    Without the need to hide from anyone,
    With just a begging bowl and few belongings,
    Dressed in garments coveted by none?

29.   And going to the charnel ground,
    When shall I compare
    My body with the dry bones there,
    So soon to fall to nothing, all alike?

30.   This form of mine, this very flesh,
    Is soon to give out such a stench
    That even jackals won't come close—
    For that indeed is all its destiny.

31.   This body, now so whole and integral,
    This flesh and bone that life has knit together,
    Will drift apart, disintegrate.
    And how much more will friend depart from friend?

32.   Alone we're born, alone we come into the world,
    And when we die, alone we pass away.
    For no one shares our fate, and none our suffering.
    So what are they to me, such "friends" and all their hindrances?

33.   Like those who journey on the road,
    Who halt and make a pause along the way,
    Beings on the pathways of the world,
    All halt, and pause, and take their birth.

34. Until the time comes round
    When four men carry me away,
    Amid the tears and sighs of worldly folk—
    Till then, I will away and go into the forest.

35. There, with no befriending or begrudging,
    I will stay alone in solitude,
    Considered from the outset as already dead,
    Thus, when I die, a source of pain to none.

36. And likewise, staying all alone,
    The sound of mourning will not hinder me.[87]
    And no one will be there distracting me
    From thinking of the Buddha and the practice.

37. Therefore in these lovely gleaming woods,
    With joy that's marred by few afflictions,
    I shall pacify all mental wandering,
    And there remain in blissful solitude.

38. Relinquishing all other aspirations,
    Focusing myself on one intent alone,
    I'll strive to still my mind,
    And, calming it, to bring it to subjection.

39. In this and every other world,
    Desire's the fertile parent of all conflict.
    Here in this world, bonds and wounds and death,
    And in the next, a hell is all prepared.

40. You send your go-betweens, both boy and maid,[88]
    With many invitations for the prize,
    Avoiding, in the quest, no sin,
    No deed that brings an ill renown,

41.   Nor acts of frightful risk,
     Nor loss and ruin of both goods and wealth—
     And all for pleasure and the perfect bliss,
     That utmost penetrating kiss

42.   Of what in truth is nothing but a heap of bones,
     Devoid of self, without its own existence!
     Is this the only object of desire and lust?
     Sooner pass beyond all suffering and grief!

43.   Oh what pains you went through just to draw the veil,
     And lift the face that modestly looked down.
     That face which, looked upon or not,
     Was always carefully concealed.[89]

44.   That face for which you languished so . . .
     Well, here it is, now nakedly exposed.
     The crows have done their work for you to see.
     What's this? You run away so soon?

45.   That body that you guarded jealously
     And shielded from the eyes of other men,
     What, miser that you are, you don't protect it,
     Now that it's the food of graveyard birds?

46.   Look, this mass of human flesh,
     Soon to be the fare of carrion beasts,
     You deck with flowers, sandalwood, and jewels,
     And yet it is the provender of others!

47.   Look again, these heaps of bones—
     Inert and dead. Why, what are you so scared of?
     Why did you not fear them when they walked around
     And moved with ease, like deadly revenants?

48. You loved them once, when clothed and draped they were.
     Well, now they're naked, why do you not want them?
     Ah, you say, your lust is no more there,
     But why did you embrace them, all bedecked and covered?

49. From food, a single source, come equally
     Their bodies' filth, the honey-nectar of their mouths.
     So why are you delighted by saliva,
     And yet revolted by their excrement?

50. Taking no delight in pillows,
     Soft though they may be to touch and stroke,
     You claim the human form emits no evil stench;
     You don't know what is clean, befooled by lust!

51. Lustful ones, befuddled by desire,
     Because you cannot copulate with them,
     You angrily find fault with pillows,
     Even though they're smooth and soft to touch!

52. And if you have no love for filth,
     How can you coddle on your lap
     A cage of bones tied fast with sinews
     Plastered over with the mud of flesh?

53. The reason is you're full of filth yourself,
     And wallow in it constantly.
     It is indeed just dirt that you desire,
     And therefore long for other sacks of filth!

54. "But it's the skin and flesh I love
     To touch and look upon."
     Then why do you not wish for flesh alone,
     Inanimate and in its natural state?

55. The mind of the beloved you so much desire
     Eludes your touch; this mind you cannot see.
     Nothing that the sense perceives is mind,
     So why indulge in pointless copulation?

56. To fail to understand the unclean nature
     Of another's flesh is not perhaps so strange.
     But not to see the filthy nature
     Of oneself is very strange indeed!

57. Why does the mind, intent on filthiness,
     Neglect the fresh young lotus blossom,
     Opened in the sunlight of a cloudless sky,
     To take joy rather in a sack of dirt?

58. And since you're disinclined to touch
     A place or object grimed with excrement,
     Why wish to touch the body
     Whence such excrement has come?

59. And if you have no craving for impurity,
     Why will you now embrace and kiss
     What comes from such an unclean place,
     Engendered likewise from an unclean seed?[90]

60. The fetid worms that live in filth—
     You have no love for them, not even little ones.
     And yet you're lusting for a human form,
     From filth arisen and replete with it!

61. Toward your own impurity
     Disgust you do not feel; but what is more,
     Attracted to the ordure of an unclean sack,
     You long to touch the body of another!

62. Pleasant substances like camphor,
    Rice, and fresh green herbs—
    Put them in your mouth and spit them out:
    The ground itself is rendered foul with it!

63. If still you doubt such filthiness,
    Though it is very plain for all to see,
    Go off into the charnel grounds, observe
    The fetid bodies there abandoned.

64. If when their skins are peeled away,
    They make you feel great horror and revulsion,
    How, having seen this, later on,
    Can you desire and crave for such an object?

65. The scent that now perfumes the skin
    Is sandalwood and nothing else.
    Yet how is it that one thing's fragrance
    Causes you to long for something else?

66. Surely it is best to cease to long
    For what by nature gives off evil smells.
    Yet worldly people's lusts are all confused—
    To what end do they daub the flesh with perfumes?

67. For if this scent in fact is sandalwood,
    How will we now describe the body's odors?
    And how is it that one thing's fragrance
    Causes you to long for something else?

68. With lanky hair, with long nails overgrown,
    With dirty teeth, and reeking with the stink of slime,
    This body, naked, as it is, untended,
    Is indeed a nightmare to behold!

69. Why go to such excess to clean and polish
    What is but a weapon that will injure us?
    The cares that people squander on themselves in ignorance
    Convulse the universe with madness.

70. Did you see the heaps of human bones
    And feel revulsion in the charnel ground?
    Then why such pleasure in your cities of the dead,
    Frequented by such skeletons that live and move?

71. What's more, possession of another's filth
    Is not to be acquired free of charge.
    All is at a price: exhaustion in this life,
    And in the next, the sufferings of hell!

72. To pay the bride-price young men are unable.
    So while they're young, what joy is there for them?
    Their lives are spent to gain sufficient wealth,
    By then they're old—too old to satisfy their lust!

73. Some are miserable as well as lustful.
    For worn out by their day-long work,
    They go home broken with fatigue,
    To sleep the slumbers of a corpse!

74. Some, obliged to travel far abroad,
    Must suffer separation from their wives,
    From children whom they love and long to see.
    They do not meet with them for years on end.

75. Some, ambitious for advancement,
    Not knowing how to get it, sell themselves.
    Happiness eludes their grasp, and pointlessly
    They live, in bondage to their masters.

76. Some completely sell themselves,
    No longer free, in slavery to others.
    And, destitute, their wives give birth
    With only trees for shelter, in the wilderness.

77. Fools ensnared by craving for a livelihood
    Decide that they will make their fortune
    In the wars, though fearful for their lives.
    And seeking gain, it's slavery they get.

78. Some, as fruits of their ambition,
    Have their bodies slashed, impaled on pointed stakes.
    Some are wounded, run through by the lance,
    While some are put to death by fire.

79. The trouble guarding what we have, the pain of losing all!
    See the endless hardships brought on us by wealth!
    Those distracted by their love of riches
    Never have a moment's rest from sorrows of existence.

80. They indeed, possessed of many wants,
    Will suffer many troubles, all for very little:
    Mouthfuls of the hay the oxen get
    As recompense for having pulled the cart!

81. The cattle's fodder!—not so very rare—
    And for the sake of such a petty thing,
    Tormented by their karma they destroy
    This precious human life so hard to find.

82. All that we desire is sure to perish,
    And afterwards we fall to hellish torment.
    The constant, minor troubles we endure
    Are all for what amounts to very little!

83. But with a millionth part of such vexation
    Enlightenment itself could be attained!
    The pains the lustful take exceed by far the trials encountered on
        the path,
    And at the end the fruit is very far from buddhahood!

84. Reflect upon the horrors of the states of sorrow!
    Weapons, poisons, fires, and yawning chasms,
    Hostile foes—these worldly pains are slight
    Compared with what we get as fruit of our desire!

85. And so, revolted by our lust and wanting,
    Let us now rejoice in solitude,
    In places where all strife and conflict cease,
    The peace and stillness of the greenwood.

86. In pleasant dwellings formed of massive stone,
    And cooled by sandal trees beneath the moon,
    In woodlands wafted by the gentle breeze,
    Our minds intent on bringing good to others,

87. In caves, beneath the trees, in houses left abandoned
    May we linger long as we might wish.
    Relinquishing the pain of guarding our possessions,
    Let us live in freedom, unconfined by cares.

88. To have such liberty unmarred by craving,
    And loosed from every bond and tie—
    A life of such contentment and such bliss,
    The gods like Indra would be pressed to find!

89. Reflecting in such ways as these,
    Upon the excellence of solitude,
    Pacify completely all discursiveness
    And cultivate the mind of bodhichitta.

90. Strive at first to meditate
    Upon the sameness of yourself and others.[91]
    In joy and sorrow all are equal.
    Thus be guardian of all, as of yourself.

91. The hand and other limbs are many and distinct,
    But all are one—one body to be kept and guarded.
    Likewise, different beings in their joys and sorrows,
    Are, like me, all one in wanting happiness.

92. My pain does not in fact afflict
    Or cause discomfort to another's body.
    Through clinging to my "I," this suffering is mine.
    And, being mine, is very hard to bear.

93. And other beings' pain
    I do not feel, and yet
    Because I take them for my own[92]
    Their suffering is likewise hard to bear.

94. And therefore I'll dispel the pain of others,
    For it is simply pain, just like my own.
    And others I will aid and benefit,
    For they are living beings, just like me.

95. Since I and other beings both,
    In wanting happiness, are equal and alike,
    What difference is there to distinguish us,
    That I should strive to have my bliss alone?

96. Since I and other beings both,
    In fleeing suffering, are equal and alike,
    What difference is there to distinguish us,
    That I should save myself and not the other?

{ 123 }

97. Since pains of others do no harm to me,
     What reason do I have to shield myself?
     But why to guard against "my" future pain which
     Does no harm to this, my present "me"?

98. To think that "I will have to suffer it"
     In fact is but a false conception—
     In the present moment, "I" will perish;
     At a later time, another will be born.

99. It's for the sufferer himself, you'll say,
     To shield himself from injuries that come!
     The pain felt in my foot is not my hand's,
     So why, in fact, does one protect the other?

100. "This may be irrational," you'll say.
     "It happens simply through the force of ego-clinging."
     But that which is illogical for both of us
     Should be refuted and dispensed with utterly!

101. Labeled continuities and aggregates,
     Like strings of beads and armies, are like mirages.
     Likewise, there is no one hurt by suffering,
     For who is there to be oppressed by it?

102. And if there is no subject suffering,
     Mine and other's pain—how are they different?
     Simply, then, since pain is pain, I will dispel it.
     What grounds have you for all your strong distinctions?

103. Thus the suffering of everyone
     Should be dispelled, and here there's no debate.
     To free myself from pain means freeing all;
     Contrariwise, I suffer with the pain of beings.

104. "The sorrow felt in pity aggravates," you say,
     "The pain already felt, so why engender it?"
     But can the sting of pity be compared
     With all that other beings have to suffer?

105. And if through such a single pain
     A multitude of sorrows can be remedied,
     Such pain as this a loving being
     Strives to foster in himself and others.

106. Even thus, Supuṣhpachandra[93]
     Knowing how the king would cause him harm
     Did nothing to escape from tribulation,
     That the pains of many should be overthrown.

107. Those whose minds are practiced in this way,
     Whose happiness it is to soothe the pain of others,
     Will venture in the hell of unremitting agony,
     As swans sweep down upon a lotus lake.

108. The oceanlike immensity of joy
     Arising when all beings will be freed,
     Will this not be enough? Will this not satisfy?
     The wish for my own freedom, what is that to me?

109. The work of bringing benefit to beings
     Will not, then, make me proud and self-admiring.
     The happiness of others is itself my satisfaction;
     I do not expect another recompense.

110. Just as I defend myself
     From all unpleasant happenings, however small,
     Likewise I shall act for others' sake
     To guard and shield them with compassion.

111. Although the drop of sperm and blood[94]
     Is alien and in itself devoid of entity,
     Yet, because of strong habituation,
     I recognize and claim it as my "I."

112. Why, then, not identify
     Another's body, calling *it* my "I"?
     And vice versa, why should it be hard,
     To think of this my body as another's?

113. Seeing then the faults that come from cherishing myself,
     The oceanic qualities that come from loving others,
     I shall lay aside all love of self
     And gain the habit of adopting others.

114. Hands and other limbs
     Are thought of as the members of a body.
     Shall we not consider others likewise—
     Limbs and members of a living whole?

115. Just as in this form, devoid of "I,"
     The thought of self arose through long habituation,
     Why, upon the aggregate of living beings,
     Should not the thought of "I," through habit, be imputed?

116. Thus when I work for others' sake,
     No reason can there be for boasting or amazement.
     For it is just as when I feed myself—
     I don't expect to be rewarded.

117. Just as I defend myself, therefore,
     From all unpleasant happenings however small,
     Likewise I shall act for others' sake
     To guard and to protect them with compassion.

118. This is why the Lord Avalokita
     Out of great compassion blessed his name,
     That those caught in the midst of multitudes
     Might be released and freed from every fear.[95]

119. And so we should be undeterred by hardships,
     For by influence of use and habit,
     People even come to grieve for one
     Whose very name strikes terror in their hearts!

120. Those desiring speedily to be
     A refuge for themselves and other beings.
     Should interchange the terms of "I" and "other,"
     And thus embrace a sacred mystery.

121. Because of our attachment to our bodies,
     We're terrified by even little things.
     This body, then, this source of so much fear—
     Who would not revile it as the worst of enemies?

122. Wishing to relieve our bodies' ills,
     Our hungry mouths, the dryness of our throats,
     We lie in wait along the road
     And steal the lives of fishes, birds, and deer.

123. And for the body's service and advantage,
     Some there are who even kill their parents,
     Or steal what has been offered to the Triple Gem,
     Because of which, they'll burn in deepest hell.

124. Where then is the prudent man
     Who wants to pamper and protect his body?
     Who will not ignore and treat with scorn
     What is for him a dangerous enemy?

125. "If I give this, what will be left for me?"
Thinking of oneself—the way of evil ghosts.
"If I keep this, what will be left to give?"
Concern for others is the way of heaven.[96]

126. If to serve myself I harm another,
I'll suffer later in the realms of hell.
If for others' sake I harm myself,
Every excellence will be my heritage.

127. Wanting what is best for me—
Stupidity and lower realms result!
Let this be changed, applied to others—
Honors and the realms of bliss will come!

128. Enslaving others, forcing them to serve me,
I will come to know the state of servitude.
But if I labor for the good of others,
Mastery and leadership will come to me.

129. All the joy the world contains
Has come through wishing happiness for others.
All the misery the world contains
Has come through wanting pleasure for oneself.

130. Is there need for lengthy explanation?
Childish beings look out for themselves,
While Buddhas labor for the good of others:
See the difference that divides them!

131. If I do not give away
My happiness for others' pain,
Enlightenment will never be attained,
And even in saṃsāra, joy will fly from me.

132. Leaving future lives outside the reckoning,
      Even this life's needs are not fulfilled[97]—
      When servants do not do their work,
      And masters do not pay the wages earned.

133. Casting far away abundant joys
      That may be gained in this or future lives,
      Because of bringing harm to other beings,
      I ignorantly bring myself intolerable pain.

134. All the harm with which this world is rife,
      All fear and suffering that there is,
      Clinging to the "I" has caused it!
      What am I to do with this great demon?

135. If this "I" is not relinquished wholly,
      Sorrow likewise cannot be avoided.
      For if he does not keep away from fire,
      A man cannot escape from being burned.

136. To free myself from harm
      And others from their sufferings,
      Let me give myself away,
      And cherish others as I love myself.

137. "For I am now beneath the rule of others,"
      Of this you must be certain, O my mind.
      And now no longer shall you have a thought
      That does not wish the benefit of beings.

138. My sight and other senses, now the property of others—
      To use them for myself would be illicit.
      How much more so is it disallowed to use
      My faculties against their rightful owners?

139. Thus others will be now my chief concern.
     And everything I see my body has
     Will all be seized and given
     For the use and service of all other beings.

140. Take others—lower, higher, equal—as yourself;[98]
     Identify yourself as "other."
     Then, without another thought,
     Experience envy, pride, and rivalry.

141. He's the center of attention; I am nothing,
     And unlike him, I'm poor without possessions.
     Everyone looks up to him, despising me;
     All goes well for him, for me there's only bitterness!

142. All I have is sweat and drudgery,
     While he's there, sitting at his ease.
     He's great, respected in the world,
     While I'm the underdog, a well-known nobody.

143. What! A nobody without distinction?
     Not true! I do have some good qualities.
     He's not the best, he's lower down than some;
     While, when compared with some, I do excel!

144. My discipline, my understanding have declined,
     But I am helpless, ruled by my defilements.
     As much as he is able, he should cure me,
     And I should be submissive even to his punishments.

145. The fact is he does nothing of the sort!
     By what right, then, does he despise me?
     What use, then, are his qualities to me,
     Those qualities of which he's so possessed?

146. Indifferent to the plight of living beings,
     Who tread the brink of evil destinies,
     He makes an outward show of virtues,
     Even sets himself among the perfect!

147. That I might excel, outstripping him,
     Him, regarded as my peer and equal!
     In contests I will certainly secure
     My fame and fortune, public renown.

148. By every means I'll advertise
     My gifts to all the world,
     Ensuring that *his* qualities
     Remain unknown, ignored by everyone.

149. My faults I will conceal, dissimulate.
     For I, not he, will be the object of devotion;
     I, not he, will gain possessions and renown;
     I will be the center of attention.

150. I will take such satisfaction
     In his shame and degradation.
     I will render him despicable,
     The butt and laughingstock of everyone.

151. People say this pitiful nonentity
     Is trying to compete with me!
     But how can he resemble me, they ask,
     In learning, beauty, wealth, or pedigree?

152. Just to hear them talk about my qualities,
     My reputation on the lips of all,
     The thrill of it sends shivers down my spine,
     The pleasure that I bask and revel in!

153. Granted, even if he does have something,
     I'm the one he's working for!
     He can keep enough just to survive,
     But with my strength I'll steal away the rest.

154. I will wear his happiness away;
     I will always hurt and injure him.
     He's the one who in saṃsāra
     Did me mischiefs by the hundreds!

155. O my mind, what countless ages
     Have you spent in working for yourself?
     And what great weariness it was,
     While your reward was only misery!

156. The truth, therefore, is this:
     That you must wholly give yourself and take the other's place.
     The Buddha did not lie in what he said—
     You'll see the benefits that come from it.

157. If, indeed, you had in former times
     Embraced this work and undertaken it,
     You could not still be lacking
     In the perfect bliss of buddhahood.

158. Just as you identify
     A drop of other's blood and sperm,
     And cling to it as though it were yourself,
     Now take sentient beings—others—as your self.

159. Now be covetous for others' sake,
     Of everything you see that you possess.
     Steal it, take it all away,
     And use it for the benefit of others.

160. I indeed am happy, others sad;
      I am high and mighty, others low;
      I am helped while others are abandoned:
      Why am I not jealous of myself?

161. Happiness, fulfillment: these I leave aside.
      The pain of others: this I will embrace.
      Inquiring of myself repeatedly,
      I will become aware of all my faults.

162. When others are at fault, I'll take
      And turn the blame upon myself.
      And all my sins, however slight,
      Confess, and make them known to many.

163. The fame of others I will magnify
      That it might thus outshine my own.
      Among them I will be as one who serves,
      My lowly labor for their benefit.

164. This ego is by nature rife with defects,
      Its accidental talents I should hide, not praise.
      Whatever qualities it has I will conceal,
      That they remain unknown to everyone.

165. All the harm, in short, my ego does
      To its advantage and to others' cost,
      May all of it descend upon itself,
      To its own hurt—to others' benefit.

166. Do not let it strut about the place,
      So arrogant, so overbearing.
      But like a newly wedded bride,
      Let it be demure and blushing, timorous and shy!

167. That's how it should be and stay!
     And if it lapses, bring it forcibly to heel
     With antidotes, and if these fail,
     Well then, apply the lash!

168. And so, O mind, if still you will refuse,
     Though you have been so lengthily advised,
     Since every evil has its roots in you,
     You are indeed now ripe for punishment!

169. The time when you could do me harm
     Is in the past, and now is here no more.
     Now I see you! Where will you escape?
     I'll bring you down, and all your haughty insolence.

170. Every thought of working for myself
     Is utterly rejected, cast aside.
     "Now that you've been sold to others,
     Stop your whining, be of service!"

171. For if, through being inattentive,
     I do not deliver you to others,
     You will hand me over, it is certain,
     To the dreadful guardians of hell.

172. For this is how so many times
     You have betrayed me, and how long I've suffered!
     Now my memory is full of rancor;
     I will crush your selfish schemes!

173. And so it is that if I want contentment,
     I should never seek to please myself.
     And likewise, if I wish to save myself,
     I'll always be the guardian of others.

174. To the extent this human form
     Is cosseted and saved from hurt,
     Just so, just so, to that degree,
     It grows so sensitive and peevish.

175. For those who fall to such a state,
     The earth itself and all it holds
     Are powerless to satisfy.
     For who can give them all they crave?

176. Their hopeless craving brings them misery,
     And evil policies invade their minds.
     While those with free, untrammeled hearts,
     Will never know an end of excellence.

177. Therefore, for the increase of my body's wants,
     I'll give no space, no opportunity.
     And of possessions, those things are the best
     That do not captivate by their attractiveness.

178. Dust and ashes are the body's final state,
     This body which, inert, is moved by other forces.
     This insupportable and unclean form—
     Why do I regard it as my "I," my "self"?

179. Alive or dead, what difference does it make?
     What good to me is this machinery?
     What difference will divide it from a clod of earth?
     Oh, why not rid myself of this conceit of "self"?

180. Through lavishing attention on this body,
     Such sorrow have I brought myself so senselessly.
     What use is all my wanting, all my hating—
     For what indeed is like a log of wood?

181. Whether I protect and pamper it,
     Or whether it is torn by beaks of carrion birds,
     This body feels no pleasure, no aversion—
     Why then do I cherish it so much?

182. Resentment when it is reviled,
     Or pleasure when it is esteemed,
     Neither of these two the body feels—
     So why do I exhaust myself?

183. Because of the appreciation, you will say,
     That others, all my friends, will have of it.
     They all appreciate the bodies that they have,
     So why do I not like them as my own?[99]

184. Therefore, free from all attachment,
     I will give this body for the benefit of beings;
     Thus, though many blemishes afflict it,
     I shall take it as my necessary tool.

185. And so, enough of all my childish ways.
     I'll follow in the footsteps of the wise,
     Recalling their advice on vigilance,
     I'll shun all sleep and mental dullness.

186. Like the buddhas' heirs, in their compassion,
     I will take the burden, all that should be borne.
     For if I do not labor night and day,
     When will all my sorrows have an end?[100]

187. Thus to banish all obscuring veils
     I'll bend my mind from the mistaken path;
     And constantly upon this perfect object
     I shall rest my mind in even meditation.

9

Wisdom[101]

1. All these branches of the Doctrine
   The Powerful Lord expounded for the sake of wisdom.
   Therefore they must generate this wisdom
   Who wish to have an end of suffering.

2. Relative and absolute,
   These the two truths are declared to be.
   The absolute is not within the reach of intellect,
   For intellect is grounded in the relative.

3. Two kinds of people are to be distinguished:
   Meditative thinkers and ordinary folk;
   The common views of ordinary people
   Are superseded by the views of meditators.

4. And within the ranks of meditators,
   The lower, in degrees of insight, are confuted by the higher.
   For all employ the same comparisons,
   And the goal, if left unanalyzed, they all accept.

5. When ordinary folk perceive phenomena,
   They look on them as real and not illusory.
   This, then, is the subject of debate
   Where ordinary and meditators differ.

6. Forms and so forth, which we sense directly,
    Exist by general acclaim, though logic disallows them.
    They're false, deceiving, like polluted substances
    Regarded in the common view as clean.

7. That he might instruct the worldly,
    Buddha spoke of "things," but these in truth
    Lack even momentariness.
    "It's wrong to claim that this is relative!"—If so you say,

8. Then know that there's no fault. For momentariness
    Is relative for meditators, but for the worldly, absolute.
    Were it otherwise, the common view
    Could fault our certain insight into corporal impurity.

9. "Through a buddha, who is but illusion, how does merit spring?"
    As if the Buddha were existing truly.
    "But," you ask, "if beings likewise are illusions,
    How, when dying, can they take rebirth?"

10. As long as the conditions are assembled,
    Illusions, likewise, will persist and manifest.
    Why, through simply being more protracted,
    Should sentient beings be regarded as more real?

11. If thus I were to slay or harm a mere mirage,
    Because there is no mind, no sin occurs.
    But beings are possessed of miragelike minds;
    Sin and merit will, in consequence, arise.

12. Spells and incantations cannot, it is true,
    Give minds to mirages, and so no mind arises.
    But illusions spring from various causes;
    The kinds of mirage, then, are likewise various—

13.   A single cause for everything there never was!
       "If, ultimately," you will now enquire,
       "Everything is said to be nirvāṇa,
       Saṃsāra, which is relative, must be the same.

14.   "Therefore even buddhahood reverts to the saṃsāric state.
       So why," you ask, "pursue the bodhisattva path?"
       As long as there's no cutting of the causal stream,
       There is no routing of illusory appearance.

15.   But when the causal stream is interrupted,
       All illusions, even relative, will cease.
       "If that which is deceived does not exist,
       What is it," you ask, "that sees illusion?"

16.   But if, for you, these same illusions have no being,
       What, indeed, remains to be perceived?
       If objects have another mode of being,
       That very mode is but the mind itself.

17.   But if the mirage is the mind itself,
       What, then, is perceived by what?
       The Guardian of the World himself has said
       That mind cannot be seen by mind.

18.   In just the same way, he has said,
       The sword's edge cannot cut the sword.
       "But," you say, "it's like the flame
       That perfectly illuminates itself."

19.   The flame, in fact, can never light itself.
       And why? Because the darkness never dims it!
       "The blueness of a blue thing," you will say,
       "Depends, unlike a crystal, on no other thing.

20. "Likewise some perceptions
     Rise from other things—while some do not."
     But what is blue has never of itself imposed
     A blueness on its nonblue self.

21. The phrase "the lamp illuminates itself"
     The mind can know and formulate.
     But what is there to know and say
     That "mind is self-illuminating"?

22. The mind, indeed, is never seen by anyone,
     And therefore, whether it can know or cannot know itself,
     Just like the beauty of a barren woman's daughter,
     This merely forms the subject of a pointless conversation.

23. "But if," you ask, "the mind is not self-knowing,
     How does it remember what it knew?"
     We say that like the poison of the water rat,
     It's from the link with outer things that memory occurs.

24. "In certain cases," you will say, "the mind
     Can see the minds of others, how then not itself?"
     But through the application of a magic balm,
     The eye may see the treasure, but the salve it does not see.

25. It's not indeed our object to disprove
     Experiences of sight or sound or knowing.
     Our aim is here to undermine the cause of sorrow:
     The thought that such phenomena have true existence.

26. "Illusions are not other than the mind," you say,
     And yet you also claim that they are not the same.
     But must they not be different if the mind is real?
     And how can mind be real if there's no difference?

27. "A mirage may be known," you say, "though lacking true
existence."
The knower is the same: it knows, but is a mirage.
"But what supports saṃsāra must be real," you say,
"Or else saṃsāra is like empty space."

28. But how could the unreal proceed to function,
Even if it rests on something real?
This mind of yours is isolated and alone,
Alone, in solitude, and unaccompanied.

29. If the mind indeed is free of objects,
All beings must be buddhas, thus gone and enlightened.
Therefore what utility or purpose can there be
In saying thus, that there is "Only Mind"?

30. Even if we know that all is like illusion,
How will this dispel afflictive passion?
Magicians may indeed themselves desire
The mirage-women they themselves create.

31. The reason is they have not rid themselves
Of habits of desiring objects of perception;
And when they gaze upon such things,
Their aptitude for emptiness is weak indeed.

32. By training in this aptitude for emptiness,
The habit to perceive substantiality will fade.
By training in the view that all lacks entity,
This view itself will also disappear.

33. "There is nothing"—when this is asserted,
No "thing" is there to be examined.
For how can nothing, lacking all support,
Remain before the mind as something present?

34. When real and nonreal both
    Are absent from before the mind,
    Nothing else remains for mind to do
    But rest in perfect peace, from concepts free.

35. As the wishing jewel and tree of miracles
    Fulfill and satisfy all hopes and wishes,
    Likewise, through their prayers for those who might be trained,
    Victorious Ones appear within the world.

36. The healing shrine of the garuḍa,
    Even when its builder was long dead,
    Continued even ages thence
    To remedy and soothe all plagues and venom.

37. Likewise, though the bodhisattva has transcended sorrow,
    By virtue of his actions for the sake of buddhahood,
    The shrines of buddha-forms appear and manifest,
    Enacting and fulfilling every deed.

38. "But how," you ask, "can offerings made
    To beings freed from all discursiveness give fruit?"
    It's said that whether buddhas live or pass beyond,
    The offerings made to them have equal merit.

39. Whether you assert the relative or ultimate,
    The scriptures say that merit will result.
    Merits will be gained regardless
    Of the Buddha's true or relative existence.

40. "We're freed," you say, "through seeing the (Four) Truths—
    What use is it to us, this view of voidness?"
    But as the scriptures have themselves proclaimed,
    Without it there is no enlightenment.

41. You say the Mahāyāna has no certainty.
    But how do you substantiate your own tradition?
    "Because it is accepted by both parties," you will say.
    But at the outset, you yourselves lacked proof!

42. The reasons why you trust in your tradition
    May likewise be applied to Mahāyāna.
    Moreover, if accord between two parties shows the truth,
    The Vedas and rest are also true.

43. "Mahāyāna is at fault," you say, "because it is contested."
    But by non-Buddhists are your scriptures also questioned,
    While other Buddhist schools impugn and spurn them.
    Therefore, your tradition you must now abandon.

44. The true monk is the very root of Dharma,
    But difficult it is to be a monk indeed.
    And hard it is for minds enmeshed in thoughts
    To pass beyond the bonds of suffering.

45. You say there's liberation in the instant
    That defilements are entirely forsaken.
    Yet those who from defilements are set free
    Continue to display the influence of karma.

46. "Only for a while," you say. "For it is certain
    That the cause of rebirth, craving, is exhausted."
    They have no craving, granted, through defiled emotion.
    But how could they avoid the craving linked with ignorance?

47. This craving is produced by virtue of sensation,
    And sensation, this they surely have.
    Concepts linger still within their minds;
    And it is to these concepts that they cling.

48. The mind that has not realized voidness,
     May be halted, but will once again arise—
     Just as from a nonperceptual absorption.
     Therefore, voidness must be cultivated.

49. If all that is encompassed by the sūtras
     You hold to be the Buddha's perfect speech,
     Why do you not hold the greater part of Mahāyāna,
     Which with your sūtras is in perfect harmony?[102]

50. If due to just a single jarring element,
     The whole is held to be at fault,
     How might not a single point in concord with the sūtras
     Vindicate the rest as Buddha's teaching?

51. Mahākāshyapa[103] himself and others
     Could not sound the depths of such a teaching.
     Who will therefore say they are to be rejected
     Just because they are not grasped by you?

52. To linger and abide within saṃsāra,
     But freed from every craving and from every fear,
     To work the benefit of those who ignorantly suffer:
     Such is the fruit that emptiness will bear.

53. From this, the voidness doctrine will be seen
     To be immune from all attack.
     And so, with every doubt abandoned,
     Let us meditate upon this emptiness.

54. Afflictive passion and the veils of ignorance—
     The cure for these is emptiness.
     Therefore, how could they not meditate upon it
     Who wish swiftly to attain omniscience?

55. Whatever is the source of pain and suffering,
    Let that be the object of our fear.
    But voidness will allay our every sorrow;
    How could it be for us a thing of dread?

56. If such a thing as "I" exists indeed,
    Then terrors, granted, will torment it.
    But since no self or "I" exists at all,
    What is there left for fears to terrify?

57. The teeth, the hair, the nails are not the "I,"
    And "I" is not the bones or blood;
    The mucus from the nose, and phlegm, are not the "I,"
    And neither is it made of lymph or pus.

58. The "I" is not the body's grease or sweat,
    The lungs and liver likewise do not constitute it.
    Neither are the inner organs "I,"
    Nor yet the body's excrement and waste.

59. The flesh and skin are not the "I,"
    And neither are the body's warmth and breath.
    The cavities within the frame are not the "I,"
    And "I" is not accounted for within the six perceptions.

60. If the hearing consciousness is permanent,
    It follows that it's hearing all the time.
    If there is no object, what is knowing what?
    Why do you now say that there is consciousness?

61. If consciousness is that which does not know,
    It follows that a stick is also conscious.
    Therefore, in the absence of a thing to know,
    It is clear that consciousness will not arise.

62. "But consciousness may turn to apprehend a form," you say.
    But why, then, does it cease to hear?
    Perhaps you say the sound's no longer there.
    If so, the hearing consciousness is likewise absent.

63. How could that which has the nature of perceiving sound
    Be changed into a form-perceiver?
    "A single man," you say, "can be both son and father."
    But these are merely names; his nature is not so.

64. Thus "pleasure," "pain," "neutrality"
    Do not partake of fatherhood or sonship,
    And we indeed have never yet observed
    A consciousness of form perceiving sound.

65. "But like an actor," you will say, "it takes on different roles."
    If so, this consciousness is not a changeless thing.
    "It's one thing," you will say, "with different modes."
    That's unity indeed, and never seen before!

66. "But different modes," you claim, "without reality."
    And so its essence you must now describe.
    You say that this is simply knowing—
    All beings therefore are a single thing.

67. What has mind and what does not have mind
    Are likewise one, for both are equal in existing.
    If the different features are deceptive,
    What is the support that underlies them?

68. Something destitute of mind, we hold, cannot be self,
    For mindlessness means matter, like a vase.
    "But," you say, "the self has consciousness, when joined to mind."
    But this refutes its nature of unconsciousness.

69. If the self, moreover, is immutable,
    What change in it could mingling with the mind produce?
    And selfhood we might equally affirm
    Of empty space, inert and destitute of mind.

70. "If," you ask, "the self does not exist,
    How can acts be linked with their results?
    If when the deed is done, the doer is no more,
    Who is there to reap the karmic fruit?"

71. The basis of the act and fruit are not the same,
    And thus a self lacks scope for its activity.
    On this, both you and we are in accord—
    What point is there in our debating?

72. A cause coterminous with its result
    Is something quite impossible to see.
    And only in the context of a single mental stream
    Can it be said that one who acts will later reap the fruit.

73. The thoughts now passed, and those to come, are not the self;
    They are no more, or are not yet.
    Is then the self the thought which now is born?
    If so, it sinks to nothing when the latter fades.

74. For instance, we may take banana trees—
    Cutting through the fibers, finding nothing.
    Likewise analytical investigation
    Will find no "I," no underlying self.

75. "If beings," you will say, "have no existence,
    Who will be the object of compassion?"
    Those whom ignorance imputes and vows to save,
    Intending thus to gain the lofty goal.

76.   "Since beings are no more," you ask, "who gains the fruit?"
       It's true! The aspiration's made in ignorance.
       But for the total vanquishing of sorrow,
       The goal, which ignorance conceives, should not be spurned.

77.   The source of sorrow is the pride of saying "I,"
       Fostered and increased by false belief in self.
       To this you may say that there's no redress,
       But meditation on no-self will be the supreme way.

78.   What we call the body is not feet or shins,
       The body, likewise, is not thighs or loins.
       It's not the belly nor indeed the back,
       And from the chest and arms the body is not formed.

79.   The body is not ribs or hands,
       Armpits, shoulders, bowels, or entrails;
       It is not the head or throat:
       From none of these is "body" constituted.

80.   If "body," step by step,
       Pervades and spreads itself throughout its members,
       Its parts indeed are present in the parts,
       But where does "body," in itself, abide?

81.   If "body," single and entire,
       Is present in the hand and other members,
       However many parts there are, the hand and all the rest,
       You'll find an equal quantity of "bodies."

82.   If "body" is not outside or within its parts,
       How is it, then, residing in its members?
       And since it has no basis other than its parts,
       How can it be said to be at all?

83.   Thus there is no "body" in the limbs,
      But from illusion does the idea spring,
      To be affixed to a specific shape—
      Just as when a scarecrow is mistaken for a man.

84.   As long as the conditions are assembled,
      A body will appear and seem to be a man.
      As long as all the parts are likewise present,
      It's there that we will see a body.

85.   Likewise, since it is a group of fingers,
      The hand itself is not a single entity.
      And so it is with fingers, made of joints—
      And joints themselves consist of many parts.

86.   These parts themselves will break down into atoms,
      And atoms will divide according to direction.
      These fragments, too, will also fall to nothing.
      Thus atoms are like empty space—they have no real existence.

87.   All form, therefore, is like a dream,
      And who will be attached to it, who thus investigates?
      The body, in this way, has no existence;
      What is male, therefore, and what is female?

88.   If suffering itself is truly real,
      Then why is joy not altogether quenched thereby?
      If pleasure's real, then why will pleasant tastes
      Not comfort and amuse a man in agony?

89.   If the feeling fails to be experienced,
      Through being overwhelmed by something stronger,
      How can "feeling" rightly be ascribed
      To that which lacks the character of being felt?

90. Perhaps you say that only subtle pain remains,
    Its grosser form has now been overmastered,
    Or rather it is felt as mere pleasure.
    But what is subtle still remains itself.

91. If, through presence of its opposite,
    Pain and sorrow fail to manifest,
    To claim with such conviction that it's felt
    Is surely nothing more than empty words.

92. Since so it is, the antidote
    Is meditation and analysis.
    Investigation and resultant concentration
    Is indeed the food and sustenance of yogīs.

93. If between the sense power and a thing
    There is a space, how will the two terms meet?
    If there is no space, they form a unity,
    And therefore, what is it that meets with what?

94. Atoms and atoms cannot interpenetrate,
    For they are equal, lacking any volume.
    But if they do not penetrate, they do not mingle;
    And if they do not mingle, there is no encounter.

95. For how could anyone accept
    That what is partless could be said to meet?
    And you must show me, if you ever saw,
    A contact taking place between two partless things.

96. The consciousness is immaterial,
    And so one cannot speak of contact with it.
    A combination, too, has no reality,
    And this we have already demonstrated.

97. Therefore, if there is no touch or contact,
    Whence is it that feeling takes its rise?
    What purpose is there, then, in all our striving,
    What is it, then, that torments what?

98. Since there is no subject for sensation,
    And sensation, too, lacks all existence,
    Why, when this you clearly understand,
    Will you not pause and turn away from craving?

99. Seeing, then, and sense of touch
    Are stuff of insubstantial dreams.
    If perceiving consciousness arises simultaneously,
    How could such a feeling be perceived?

100. If the one arises first, the other after,
    Memory occurs and not direct sensation.
    Sensation, then, does not perceive itself,
    And likewise, by another it is not perceived.

101. The subject of sensation has no real existence,
    Thus sensation, likewise, has no being.
    What damage, then, can be inflicted
    On this aggregate deprived of self?

102. The mind within the senses does not dwell;
    It has no place in outer things, like form,
    And in between, the mind does not abide:
    Not out, not in, not elsewhere can the mind be found.

103. Something not within the body, and yet nowhere else,
    That does not merge with it nor stand apart—
    Something such as this does not exist, not even slightly.
    Beings have nirvāṇa by their nature.

104. If consciousness precedes the cognized object,
     With regard to what does it arise?
     If consciousness arises with its object,
     Again, regarding what does it arise?

105. If consciousness comes later than its object,
     Once again, from what does it arise?
     Thus the origin of all phenomena
     Lies beyond the reach of understanding.

106. "If this is so," you say, "the relative will cease,
     And then the two truths—what becomes of them?
     If relative depends on beings' minds,
     This means nirvāṇa is attained by none."

107. This relative is just the thoughts of beings;
     That is not the relative of beings in nirvāṇa.
     If thoughts come after this, then that is still the relative;
     If not, the relative has truly ceased.

108. Analysis and what is to be analyzed
     Are linked together, mutually dependent.
     It is on the basis of conventional consensus,
     That all examination is expressed.

109. "But when the process of analysis
     Is made in turn the object of our scrutiny,
     This investigation, likewise, may be analyzed,
     And thus we find an infinite regress."

110. If phenomena are truly analyzed,
     No basis for analysis remains.
     Deprived of further object, it subsides.
     That indeed is said to be nirvāṇa.

111. Those who say that "both are true"
    Are hard pressed to maintain their case.
    If consciousness reveals the truth of things,
    By what support is consciousness upheld?

112. If objects show that consciousness exists,
    What, in turn, upholds the truth of objects?
    If both subsist through mutual dependence,
    Both thereby will lose their true existence.

113. If, without a son, a man cannot be father;
    Whence, indeed, will such a son arise?
    There is no father in the absence of a son.
    Just so, the mind and object have no true existence.

114. "The plant arises from the seed," you say,
    "So why should not the seed be thence inferred?
    Consciousness arises from the object—
    How does it not show the thing's existence?"

115. A consciousness that's different from the plant itself
    Deduces the existence of the seed.
    But what will show that consciousness exists,
    Whereby the object is itself established?

116. At times direct perception of the world
    Perceives that all things have their causes.
    The different segments of the lotus flower
    Arise from similar diversity of causes.

117. "But what gives rise," you ask, "to such diversity of causes?"
    An ever earlier variety of cause, we say.
    "And how," you ask, "do certain fruits derive from certain
        causes?"
    Through the power, we answer, of preceding causes.

118. If Ishvara is held to be the cause of beings,
     You must now define for us his nature.
     If, by this, you simply mean the elements,
     No need to tire ourselves disputing names!

119. Yet earth and other elements are many,
     Impermanent, inert, without divinity.
     Trampled underfoot, they are impure,
     And thus they cannot be a God Omnipotent.

120. The Deity cannot be Space—inert and lifeless.
     He cannot be the Self, for this we have refuted.
     He's inconceivable, they say. Then likewise his creatorship.
     Is there any point, therefore, to such a claim?

121. What is it he wishes to create?
     Has he made the self and all the elements?
     But are not self and elements and he, himself, eternal?
     And consciousness, we know, arises from its object;

122. Pain and pleasure have, from all time, sprung from karma,
     So tell us, what has this Divinity produced?
     And if Creation's cause is unoriginate,
     How can origin be part of the result?

123. Why are creatures not created constantly,
     For Ishvara relies on nothing but himself?
     And if there's nothing that he has not made,
     What remains on which he might depend?

124. If Ishvara *depends*, the cause of all
     Is prior circumstances, and no longer he.
     When these obtain, he cannot but create;
     When these are absent, he is powerless to make.

125. If Almighty God does not intend,
     But yet creates, another thing has forced him.
     If he wishes to create, he's swayed by his desire.
     Even though Creator, then, what comes of his Omnipotence?

126. Those who say that atoms are the permanent foundation
     Have indeed already been refuted.
     The Sāṃkhyas are the ones who hold
     The Primal Substance as enduring cause.

127. "Pleasure," "pain," "neutrality," so-called,
     Are qualities which, when they rest
     In equilibrium, are termed the Primal Substance.
     The universe arises when they are disturbed.

128. Three natures in a unity are disallowed;
     This unity, therefore, cannot exist.
     These qualities, likewise, have no existence,
     For they must also be assigned a triple nature.

129. If these qualities have no existence,
     A thing like sound is very far from plausible!
     And cloth, and other mindless objects,
     Cannot be the seat of feelings such as pleasure.

130. "But," you say, "these things possess the nature of their cause."
     But have we not investigated "things" already?
     For you the cause is pleasure and the like,
     But from pleasure, cloth has never sprung!

131. Pleasure, rather, is produced from cloth,
     But this is nonexistent, therefore pleasure likewise.
     As for permanence of pleasure and the rest—
     Well, there's a thing that's never been observed.

132. If pleasure and the rest are true existents,
     Why are they not constantly perceived?
     And if you claim they take on subtle form,
     How can coarseness change, transforming into subtlety?

133. If coarseness is abandoned, subtlety assumed,
     Such transition indicates impermanence.
     Why then not accept that, in this way,
     All things will have the character of transience?

134. If you say the coarser aspect is itself the pleasure,
     The manifest sensation is of course impermanent.
     And what does not exist in any sense,
     Because it has no being, cannot manifest.

135. You do not intend that what is manifest
     Lacked earlier existence—yet this is the meaning.
     And if results exist within their cause,
     Those who eat their food, consume their excrement.

136. And likewise with the money they would spend on clothing,
     Let them rather buy the cotton grain to wear.
     "But," you say, "the world is ignorant and blind."
     Since this is taught by *those who know the truth,*

137. This knowledge must be present in the worldly.
     And if they have it, why do they not see?
     You say, "The views of worldly folk are false."
     Therefore, what they clearly see has no validity.

138. "But if there is no truth in their cognition,
     All that it assesses is perforce deceptive.
     Meditation on the supreme truth of voidness
     Ceases, therefore, to have any meaning."

139. If there is no object for analysis,
      There can be no grasping of its nonexistence.
      Therefore, a deceptive object of whatever kind
      Will also have a voidness equally deceptive.

140. Thus, when in a dream, a child has died,
      The state of mind which thinks he is no more
      Will overwhelm the thought that he was living.
      And yet, both thoughts are equally deceptive.

141. Therefore, as we see through such investigation,
      Nothing is that does not have a cause;
      And nothing is existent in its causes
      Taken one by one or in the aggregate.

142. It does not come from somewhere else,
      Neither does it stay, nor yet depart.
      How will what confusion takes for truth
      In any sense be different from a mirage?

143. Things, then, bodied forth by magic spells,
      And that which is displayed by dint of causes—
      "Whence have these arisen?" we should ask;
      And where they go to, that we should examine!

144. What arises through the meeting of conditions
      And ceases to exist when these are lacking,
      Is artificial like the mirror image;
      How can true existence be ascribed to it?

145. Something that exists with true existence—
      What need is there for it to have a cause?
      Something that is wholly inexistent—
      Again, what need has it to have a cause?

146. Even by a hundred million causes,
     No transformation is there in nonentity.
     For if this keeps its status, how could entity occur?
     And likewise, what is there that could so change?

147. When nonbeing prevails, if there's no being,
     When could being ever supervene?
     For insofar as entity does not occur,
     Nonentity itself will not depart.

148. And if nonentity is not dispersed,
     No chance is there for entity to manifest.
     Being cannot change and turn to nonbeing,
     Otherwise it has a double nature.

149. Thus there is no being,
     Likewise no cessation.
     Therefore beings, each and every one,
     Are unborn and are never ceasing.

150. Wandering beings, thus, resemble dreams
     And also the banana tree, if you examine well.
     No difference is there, in their own true nature,
     Between the states of suffering and beyond all sorrow.

151. Thus, with things devoid of true existence,
     What is there to gain, and what to lose?
     Who is there to pay me court and honors,
     And who is there to scorn and to revile me?

152. Pain and pleasure, whence do these arise?
     And what is there to give me joy and sorrow?
     In this quest and search for perfect truth,
     Who is craving, what is there to crave?

153. Examine now this world of living beings:
Who is there therein to pass away?
What is there to come, and what has been?
And who, indeed, are relatives and friends?

154. May beings like myself discern and grasp
That all things have the character of space!
But those who long for happiness and ease,
Through disputes or the cause of pleasures,

155. Are deeply troubled, or else thrilled with joy.
They suffer, strive, contend among themselves,
Slashing, stabbing, injuring each other:
They live their lives engulfed in many evils.

156. From time to time they surface in the states of bliss,
Abandoning themselves to many pleasures.
But dying, down they fall to suffer torment,
Long, unbearable, in realms of sorrow.

157. Many are the chasms and abysses of existence,
Where the truth of voidness is not found.
All is contradiction, all denial,
Suchness, or its like, can find no place.

158. There, exceeding all description,
Is the shoreless sea of pain unbearable.
Here it is that strength is low,
And lives are flickering and brief.

159. All activities for sake of life and health,
Relief of hunger and of weariness,
Time consumed in sleep, all accident and injury,
And sterile friendships with the childish—

160. Thus life passes quickly, meaningless.
     True discernment—hard it is to have!
     How then shall we ever find the means
     To curb the futile wanderings of the mind?

161. Further, evil forces work and strain
     To cast us headlong into states of woe;
     Manifold are false, deceptive trails,
     And it is hard to dissipate our doubts.

162. Hard it is to find again this state of freedom,
     Harder yet to come upon enlightened teachers,
     Hard, indeed, to turn aside the torrent of defilement!
     Alas, our sorrows fall in endless streams!

163. Sad it is indeed that living beings,
     Carried on the flood of bitter pain,
     However terrible their plight may be,
     Do not perceive they suffer so!

164. Some there are who bathe themselves repeatedly,
     And afterwards they scorch themselves with fire,
     Suffering intensely all the while,
     Yet there they stay, proclaiming loud their bliss.

165. Likewise there are some who live and act
     As though old age and death will never come to them.
     But then life's over and there comes
     The dreadful fall into the states of loss.

166. When shall I be able to allay and quench
     The dreadful heat of suffering's blazing fires,
     With plenteous rains of my own bliss
     That pour torrential from my clouds of merit?

167. My wealth of merit gathered in,
     With reverence but without conceptual aim,
     When shall I reveal this truth of emptiness
     To those who go to ruin through belief in substance?

Dedication

1.   By all the virtue I have now amassed
   By composition of this book, which speaks
   Of entry to the bodhisattva way,
   May every being tread the path to buddhahood.

2.   May beings everywhere who suffer
   Torment in their minds and bodies
   Have, by virtue of my merit,
   Joy and happiness in boundless measure.

3.   As long as they may linger in saṃsāra,
   May their present joy know no decline,
   And may they taste of unsurpassed beatitude
   In constant and unbroken continuity.

4.   Throughout the spheres and reaches of the world,
   In hellish states wherever they may be,
   May beings fettered there, tormented,
   Taste the bliss and peace of Sukhāvatī.[104]

5.   May those caught in the freezing ice be warmed.
   And from the massing clouds of bodhisattvas' prayers
   May torrents rain in boundless streams
   To cool those burning in infernal fires.

6. May forests where the leaves are blades and swords
   Become sweet groves and pleasant woodland glades.
   And may the trees of miracles appear,
   Supplanting those upon the hill of shālmali.[105]

7. And may the very pits of hell be sweet
   With fragrant pools all perfumed with the scent of lotuses,
   Be lovely with the cries of swan and goose
   And water fowl so pleasing to the ear.

8. May fiery coals turn into heaps of jewels,
   The burning ground become a crystal floor,
   The crushing hills celestial abodes,
   Adorned with offerings, the dwelling place of buddhas.

9. May the hail of lava, fiery stones, and weapons
   Henceforth become a rain of blossom.
   May those whose hell it is to fight and wound
   Be turned to lovers offering their flowers.

10. And those engulfed in fiery Vaitaraṇī,
    Their flesh destroyed, their bones bleached white as kunda flowers,
    May they, through all my merit's strength, have godlike forms,
    And sport with goddesses in Mandākinī's peaceful streams.[106]

11. "What fear is it," they'll ask, "that grips the henchmen of the
        Deadly Lord, the frightful vultures and the carrion crows?
    What noble strength is it that brings us joy and drives away our
        dreadful night?"
    And looking skyward they will see the shining form of Vajrapāṇi.
    Then may their sins be quenched in joy, and may they go to him.

12. And when they see the seething lava-flood of hell
    Extinguished in a rain of blossoms, drenched in scented water,
    At once fulfilled in bliss, they'll ask, "How can this be?"
    And thus the denizens of hell will see the One Who Holds the
        Lotus.[107]

13. "Friends, throw away your fears and quickly gather here.
For who is it who comes to banish dread, this youth with bound
     up, gleaming hair,
This loving bodhisattva saving and protecting every being,
Whose power relieves all pain, increasing joy?

14. "Do you see the splendor of his house that echoes praises of a
     thousand goddesses,
The hundred gods who lay their diadems before his lotus feet,
The rain of flowers falling on his head, his eyes moist with
     compassion?"
Thus may those in hell cry out on seeing Mañjughoṣha.

15. And likewise when, through these my roots of virtue,
They see the joyful clouds let fall their cooling scented rain,
Their obscurations cleansed by bodhisattvas like Samantabhadra,
May all those languishing in hell come now to perfect happiness.

16. And may the stooping animals be freed
From fear of being preyed upon, each other's food.
And may the famished spirits have such joy
As those who dwell within the northern continent.[108]

17. And may they be replete and satisfied
By streams of milk that pour
From noble Lord Avalokita's hand,
And bathing in it, may they be refreshed and cooled.

18. And may the blind receive their sight,
And may the deaf begin to hear,
And women near their time bring forth
Like Māyādevī,[109] free from any pain.

19. And may the naked now be clothed,
And all the hungry eat their fill.
And may those parched with thirst receive
Pure waters and delicious drink.

20. May the poor and destitute find wealth,
    The haggard and the careworn, joy.
    May confidence relieve those in despair
    And bring them steadfastness and every excellence.

21. May every being ailing with disease
    Be freed at once from every malady.
    May all the sickness that afflicts the living
    Be instantly and permanently healed.

22. May those who go in dread have no more fear.
    May captives be unchained and now set free.
    And may the weak receive their strength.
    May living beings help each other in kindness.

23. May travelers upon the road
    Find happiness no matter where they go,
    And may they gain, without the need of toil,
    The goals on which they set their hearts.

24. May those who put to sea in boat or ship
    Attain the ports that they desire,
    And may they safely come to shore
    And sweet reunion with their kith and kin.

25. May those who lose their way and stray
    In misery, find fellow travelers,
    And safe from threat of thieves and savage beasts,
    Be tireless, and their journey light.

26. May children and the old, the weak, protectorless,
    Bewildered in the wild and pathless wastes,
    And those whose minds are dulled, and all who are insane,
    Have pure celestial beings as their guardians.

27.   May all attain the human state,
       And be possessed of wisdom, faith, and love.
       With perfect livelihood and sustenance,
       May they have mindfulness throughout their lives.

28.   May everyone have unrestricted wealth,
       Just like the treasury of space,
       Enjoying it according to their wish,
       Without a trace of harm or enmity.

29.   May beings destitute of splendor,
       Become magnificent and bright.
       And those worn down by toil and drudgery
       Acquire great beauty and perfection.

30.   May all the women in this world
       Attain the strength of masculinity.[110]
       And may the lowly come to excellence,
       The proud and haughty lose their arrogance.

31.   And thus by all the merit I have gained,
       May every being, leaving none aside,
       Abandon all their evil ways
       Embracing goodness now and ever more.

32.   From bodhichitta may they never separate,
       And constantly engage in bodhisattva deeds.
       And may they be accepted as disciples by the buddhas,
       And turn aside from what is demons' work.

33.   And may these beings, each and every one,
       Enjoy an unsurpassed longevity.
       Living always in contentment,
       May the very name of death be strange to them.

34. On every side, in all the ten directions,
    May groves of wish-fulfilling trees abound,
    Resounding with the sweetness of the Teachings,
    Spoken by the buddhas and their bodhisattva children.

35. And may the earth be wholesome everywhere,
    Free from boulders, cliffs, and chasms,
    Flat and even like a level palm
    And smooth like lapis lazuli.

36. And for many circles of disciples,
    May multitudes of bodhisattvas
    Rise in every land,
    Adorning them with every excellence.

37. From bird song and the sighing of the trees,
    From shafts of light and from the sky itself,
    May living beings, each and every one,
    Perceive the constant sound of Dharma.

38. May they come into the presence of the buddhas,
    And meet with bodhisattvas, offspring of the same.
    With clouds of offerings unbounded,
    May the teachers of the world be worshiped.

39. May kindly spirits bring the rains on time,
    For harvests to be rich and plentiful.
    May princes rule according to the Truth,
    And may the world be blessed with all prosperity.

40. May medicines be strong and full of virtue;
    May healing spells be chanted with success.
    May spirits of the air that feed on flesh
    Be kind, their minds imbued with pity.

41. And let no being ever suffer pain;
    Let them neither ail nor languish, never doing evil.
    May they have no fear, nor suffer insults,
    And may their minds be ever free from sorrow.

42. In monasteries, temples, and the like,
    May reading and reciting widely flourish.
    May harmony prevail among the Saṅgha,
    And may its purpose be all fulfilled.

43. May ordained monks intent upon the practice
    Find perfect places for retreat in solitude,
    Abandon every vagrant thought,
    And meditate with trained and serviceable minds.

44. May nuns have all their wants supplied;
    May quarreling, vindictiveness be strange to them.
    Let all who have embraced monastic life
    Uphold a pure and unimpaired observance.

45. May they feel regret when discipline is broken,
    And always may they strive to cleanse away their faults.
    May they thus obtain a fortunate rebirth,
    Wherein to undertake unfailing discipline.

46. May the wise and learned be revered
    And always be sustained by offerings.
    With minds suffused with purity,
    May their renown spread far and wide.

47. May beings never languish in the lower realms;
    May pain and hardship be unknown to them.
    Enjoying more than godlike strength and beauty,
    May buddhahood for them be swiftly gained.

48. Again and yet again may sentient beings
    Make offerings to all the buddhas.
    And with Buddha's unimagined bliss
    May they enjoy undimmed and constant happiness.

49. May all the bodhisattvas now fulfill
    Their high intention for the sake of beings,
    And sentient beings likewise now receive
    The good the buddhas have in store for them.

50. And may the arhats and pratyekabuddhas
    At length attain their perfect happiness.

51. And may I also, through Mañjushrī's kindness,
    Reach the ground of Perfect Joy,[111]
    And throughout the stream of all my lives
    Embrace monastic ordination.

52. Thus may I abide, sustained
    By simple, ordinary fare.
    And in every life obtain
    A dwelling place in perfect solitude.

53. Whenever I desire to gaze on him
    Or put to him the slightest question,
    May I behold the unobstructed vision
    Of Mañjughoṣha, my protector.

54. To satisfy the needs of beings
    Dwelling in the ten directions, to the margins of the sky,
    May I reflect in every deed
    The perfect exploits of Mañjushrī.

55. And now as long as space endures,
    As long as there are beings to be found,
    May I continue likewise to remain
    To drive away the sorrows of the world.

56.   The pains and sorrows of all wandering beings—
       May they ripen wholly on myself.
       And may the virtuous company of bodhisattvas
       Bring about the happiness of beings.

57.   May the Doctrine, only remedy for suffering,
       The source of every bliss and happiness,
       Be nurtured and upheld with reverence,
       And throughout a vast continuance of time, endure!

58.   And now to Mañjughoṣha I prostrate,
       Whose kindness is the wellspring of my good intent.
       And to my virtuous friends I also bow,
       Whose inspiration gave me strength to grow.

APPENDIXES

APPENDIX I

The Life of Shāntideva

Generally speaking, our main sources for the life of Shāntideva are the Tibetan historians Butön[112] and Jetsun Tāranātha.[113] In addition, a short account (apparently a combination and abbreviation of the previous two) is to be found in the writings of the eighteenth-century Tibetan scholar Yeshe Peljor,[114] and more recent scholarship has brought to light a short Sanskrit life of Shāntideva preserved in a fourteenth-century Nepalese manuscript.[115] The following account is taken from The Nectar of Manjushri's Speech, *a commentary on* The Way of the Bodhisattva *by Khenchen Kunzang Palden, who has followed Butön closely, preferring him to Tāranātha, whose account, however, he must have known.[116]*

The author of the *Bodhicharyāvatāra* was the great master and noble bodhisattva Shāntideva. Possessing in perfect measure the three qualifications for composing shāstras,[117] Shāntideva was accepted and blessed by the venerable Mañjushrī and was adorned with seven wonderful accomplishments. It was said of him that

> He pleased the supreme yidam deity,
> And at Nālandā gave most excellent instructions.
> Victorious in debate, he worked great wonders,
> And took as his disciples beggars, kings, and nonbelievers.

The great Shāntideva was born in the southern country of Saurās-tra.[118] He was the son of the king, Kalyāṇavarman, and had the name of Shāntivarman. From his earliest youth he was devoted to the Buddha and, having a natural affinity for the Mahāyāna, he held the teachers of religion and the monastic order in great respect. He was a benefactor to all, masters and servants alike, and he cared most tenderly for the lowly, the sick, and the destitute. With his heart fixed solely upon the ways of enlightenment, he became expert in every art and science. In particular, he requested the *Tikṣhṇa-mañjushrī-sādhana*[119] from a certain ascetic mendicant. He practiced this and beheld the yidam deity.

When at length the king, his father, died, it was decided that the royal power should be conferred on Shāntivarman, and a great throne made of precious substances was duly set in place. But in his dreams that night, the prince saw Mañjushrī sitting on the very throne that he was himself to ascend the following day. Mañjushrī spoke to him and said:

My dear and only son, this is my throne,
And I, Mañjushrī, am your spiritual friend.
It is not right that you and I should take
An equal place and sit upon one seat.

With that, Shāntivarman woke from his dream and understood that it would be wrong for him to assume the kingship. Feeling no desire for the great wealth of the realm, he departed and entered the glorious monastery of Nālandā where he received ordination from Jayadeva, the chief of its five hundred paṇḍitas, taking the name of Shāntideva.[120]

Inwardly and in secret, he received the teachings of the entire Tri-piṭaka from Mañjushrī. He meditated upon them and condensed their precious contents into two shāstras: the *Digest of All Disciplines (Shikshā-samuchchaya)* and the *Digest of the Sūtras (Sūtrasamuchchaya).*[121] But though he gained mastery in the boundless qualities of abandonment and realization, the other monks knew nothing of this; and since to all outward appearances his behavior seemed to be restricted to the activi-ties of eating (*bhuj*), sleeping (*sup*), and pottering around (*kuṭīm gata*), they gave him the nickname of *Bhu-su-ku.* Such was their estimate of his outward conduct. "This man," they complained, "performs none of the three duties[122] required of the monks of this monastery. He has no right to enjoy the food and alms offered in religion to the Saṅgha. We must drive him away!"

Their plan was to take it in turns to expound the scriptures so that, when Shāntideva's turn came around, he would be embarrassed and escape. Again and again they requested him to preach, but each time he declined, saying that he was completely ignorant. They therefore asked the abbot to command him. The abbot did so, and at once Shāntideva promised to give a teaching. At this, a few of the monks began to have misgivings, not knowing what to think. So in order to put him to the test, they arranged a great quantity of offerings on the ground outside the monastery. They invited a large congregation of people, setting up an enormously high lion throne[123] in their midst. They then summoned Shāntideva; and most of the monks were thrown into a confusion when they suddenly caught sight of him sitting high up on the throne, not knowing quite how he had managed to ascend it.

"Would you like me to expound the teaching of a former scholar?" asked Shāntideva. "Or would you prefer me to recite something you have never heard before?"

Everyone was thunderstruck. "Please teach us something completely new," they said.

Now, the *Shikṣhāsamuchchaya* is too long, while the *Sūtrasamuchchaya* is too short; and so Shāntideva expounded the *Bodhicharyāvatāra*, which, though vast in meaning, is compendious in expression. The noble Mañjushrī appeared, seated in the sky, and many of the people saw him and had great faith. Even more remarkable, when Shāntideva came to the beginning of verse 34 of the ninth chapter ("When real and nonreal both are absent from before the mind . . ."), he and Mañjushrī began to rise higher and higher into the sky until at last they disappeared. Shāntideva's voice, however, continued to resound so that the commentary was completed.

Those in the congregation who possessed extraordinary powers of memory wrote down the teaching as they had apprehended it; but they produced texts of varying length: some of seven hundred verses, some of a thousand, and some of even more. The paṇḍitas of Kashmir produced a text of seven hundred verses in nine chapters, while those of central India (Magadha) came up with a text of a thousand verses in ten chapters. Disagreement and uncertainty reigned. Moreover, it had been said in the course of the recitation[124] that one should consult the *Shikshāsamuchchaya* often, and the shorter *Sūtrasamuchchaya* from time to time: two texts hitherto unknown.

At length, it was discovered that Shāntideva was living in the south, at the stūpa of Shrīdakṣhiṇa.[125] Two of the paṇḍitas who had supernormal powers of memory went to see him, intending to invite him back. But when they met him, it proved inconvenient for Shāntideva to return. Nevertheless, in answer to their inquiries, he affirmed that the length of the original text corresponded to what the scholars of Magadha had produced. As for the *Shikshāsamuchchaya* and the *Sūtrasamuchchaya*, he said that they would find both texts written in a fine scholarly hand and hidden in the roof beam of his monastic cell at Nālandā. He then instructed the two paṇḍitas, giving them explanations and transmission.

Shāntideva later traveled to the east where, through a demonstration of miraculous power, he resolved a serious controversy, establishing harmony between the contending parties and creating an atmosphere of general satisfaction.

He also accepted as his disciples a group of five hundred people, holders of outlandish non-Buddhist opinions, who were living not far to the west of Magadha. A great natural disaster had occurred, and the people were tormented by famine. They told Shāntideva that if he could save their lives, they would respect his teachings. The master filled his begging bowl with rice and, blessing it with profound concentration, fed and satisfied them all. Turning them from their uncouth ideas, he introduced them to the Buddha's Doctrine.

Sometime afterward, in the course of another terrible famine, he restored to life and health at least a thousand beggars who were emaciated and dying of starvation.

Later, Shāntideva became a bodyguard of the king of Arivishana (in Magadha) in the east. Meditating upon himself as inseparable from Mañjushrī, he took a wooden sword and imbued it with such tremendous power of Dharma that, so armed, he was able to subdue any and every onslaught. He brought about such harmony that he became the object of universal respect. Some people were, however, intensely jealous of him and protested to the king. "This man is an imposter!" they cried. "We demand an inquiry. How could he possibly have defended you? He has no weapon other than a wooden sword!"

The king was enraged and the weapons were examined one by one. When Shāntideva was ordered to take out his sword, he replied that it would be wrong to do so since it would injure the king.

"Even if it harms me," said the king, "take it out!"

Going with him to a solitary place, Shāntideva requested the king to cover one of his eyes with his hand and to look with the other. With that, the sword was drawn, and its brightness was so intense that the king's eye shot from his brow and fell to the ground. He and his escort were overcome with terror and begged Shāntideva for forgiveness, asking him for refuge. Shāntideva placed the eye back into its socket, and through his blessings the king's sight was painlessly restored. The whole country was inspired with faith and embraced the Dharma.

Later on, Shāntideva went to Shrīparvata in the south. There he took to the life of the naked Ucchushma beggars and sustained himself on the water thrown away after the washing of dishes and cooking pots. It happened that a serving woman of the king of Khatavihāra, by name Kachalahā, once saw that if any of the washing water splashed on Shāntideva as she was pouring it out, it was as if it had fallen on red hot iron. It would boil and hiss. Now, at that time, a Hindu teacher called Shaṅkaradeva appealed to the king and issued the following challenge. He said that he would draw the maṇḍala of Maheshvara[126] in the sky and that if the Buddhist teachers were unable to destroy it, then all Buddhist images and writings should be consigned to the flames, and everyone obliged to accept the tenets of his religion. The king convoked the Buddhist Saṅgha and implored them to do something. But they were powerless to destroy the maṇḍala. The king was deeply troubled, but when the serving woman told him what she had seen, he ordered that Shāntideva be summoned. They searched high and low and eventually found him sitting under a tree. When they explained the situation, he announced that he was equal to the challenge but that he would need a jug filled with water, two pieces of cloth, and fire. Everything was prepared according to his instructions. On the evening of the following day, the Hindu yogī drew some lines on the sky and departed. Everyone began to feel afraid. But early next morning, as the maṇḍala was being drawn, no sooner was the east gate finished than Shāntideva entered into a profound concentration. At once there arose a tremendous hurricane. The maṇḍala was swept away into the void; the crops, trees, and even the cities themselves were on the brink of devastation. The people were scattered; the false guru was caught up in the wind like a little bird and swept away, and a great darkness fell over the land. But from Shāntideva's brow a light burst forth showing the way for the king and queen. They had been stripped of their clothes and were covered with dust. And so with the fire he warmed them, with the water he washed them, and with the cloth he dressed and comforted them. When, through the power of Shāntideva's concentration, the people had been gathered together, washed, anointed, clothed, and set at ease, many of them entered the Doctrine of the Buddha. The heathen places of worship were demolished, and Buddhist temples built. Shāntideva propagated the teachings and caused them to remain to such an extent that the country became known as the place where false doctrine was destroyed.

❀ Historical Note

In his *Tattvasiddhi*,[127] Shāntarakṣhita, the celebrated Indian master invited to Tibet by King Trisong Detsen, quotes an entire stanza from the *Bodhicharyāvatāra* (1:10). This shows that Shāntideva must have been well known before 763 when Shāntarakṣhita first visited Tibet. Thus we have a final date, while an initial date is supplied by the seventh-century Chinese pilgrim I-tsing, who compiled an exhaustive list of all the most important Mādhyamika masters of his time. He makes no mention of Shāntideva (or, for that matter, Jayadeva), thus indicating that the author of the *Bodhicharyāvatāra* had not yet been born, or at least was still unknown, by the year 685, when I-tsing returned to China. We can therefore say with a fair degree of certainty that Shāntideva flourished in the first half of the eighth century.

It is interesting to reflect also that not only was the *Bodhicharyāvatāra* widely acclaimed in India (Butön says that more than a hundred commentaries were composed on it in Sanskrit alone),[128] but it was translated almost immediately into Tibetan by Kawa Peltsek.[129] This is in itself a remarkable circumstance and indicates the speed with which the *Bodhicharyāvatāra* had established itself as a text of major importance. It will be remembered that, like Shāntideva, Shāntarakshita was also from the monastery of Nālandā; and we may justifiably speculate that he looked upon the work of his illustrious confrère as a valuable tool in the propagation of the Mahāyāna in Tibet. Moreover, the historical proximity between the Indian master and his Tibetan translator makes it quite plausible that accurate details of Shāntideva's life might have passed into Tibetan tradition. Admittedly, Butön is writing at a distance of four centuries, and his account is brief and hagiographical, but he must have had his sources. And if these derive from ancient Tibetan records, it is at least reasonable to conclude that details in his biography of Shāntideva may not be as fanciful as modern scholarship tends to suppose.

In any case, certain indisputable facts emerge and are confirmed elsewhere. We know that Shāntideva was a monk, at least for part of his life and certainly at the time when he composed the *Bodhicharyāvatāra*. There is no reason to doubt that he was ordained at Nālandā, the principal seat of Mādhyamika philosophy. We know too that he composed three works: his masterpiece the *Bodhicharyāvatāra,* the *Shikshāsamuchchaya,* and the *Sūtrasamuchchaya.*[130] The tantric trajectory of Shāntideva's life should be noted. Granted, there is no hint of tantric teaching in either the *Bodhicharyāvatāra* or *Shikshāsamuchchaya,* but the gist of the traditional account, which is credible enough, tends to support the attribution to Shāntideva of a number of tantric texts translated into Tibetan and preserved in the Tengyur.

Appendix 2

Equalizing Self and Other

The following passage is taken from The Nectar of Mañjushrī's Speech *by Khenchen Kunzang Palden. It explains verses 90 to 98 of chapter 8, giving the metaphysical basis for the meditation on equality of self and other, and thus the whole practice of compassion according to Mahāyāna Buddhism. At the same time it throws interesting light on the Buddhist teaching on reincarnation and karma (subjects frequently misunderstood), and shows how these doctrines are consonant with the view of egolessness and nonsubstantiality.*

Two things are to be practiced on the level of relative bodhichitta: meditation on the equality of self and other, and meditation on the exchange of self and other. Without training in the former, the latter is impossible.[90] This is why Shāntideva says that we should first meditate strenuously on equality of self and other; for without it, a perfectly pure altruistic attitude cannot arise.

All beings, ourselves included, are in exactly the same predicament of wanting to be happy and not wanting to suffer. For this reason we must vigorously train in ways to develop the intention to protect others as much as ourselves, creating happiness and dispelling suffering. And this is possible, despite what we might think.

Although they have no ultimate grounds for doing so, all beings think in terms of "I" and "mine." Because of this, they conceive of

{ *180* }

"other," fixing on it as something alien, although this too is unfounded. Aside from being merely mental imputations, "I" and "other" are totally unreal. They are both illusory. Moreover, when the nonexistence of "I" is realized, the notion of "other" also disappears, for the simple reason that the two terms are posited only in relation to each other. Just as it is impossible to cut the sky in two with a knife, likewise, when the spacelike quality of egolessness is realized, it is no longer possible to make a separation between "I" and "other," and there arises an attitude of wanting to protect others as oneself, and to protect all that belongs to them with the same care as if it were one's own. As it is said, "Whoever casts aside the ordinary, trivial view of 'self' will discover the profound meaning of great 'selfhood.' "[131] Thus, for the realization of the equality of "I" and "other," it is essential to grasp that "I" and "other" are mental imputations without ultimate reality. This vital point of egolessness is difficult to understand, difficult even for a person of great acuity. Thus, as the teachings say, it is of great importance that egolessness be clearly demonstrated and assimilated.

The way to reflect on equality is as follows. [91] We can distinguish the parts of the body: hands, feet, head, inner organs, and so forth. They form a collection of distinct items, and yet, in a moment of danger, we protect them all, not wanting any of them to suffer. We regard them all as a single body to be protected. We think, "This is my body," and we cling to it and take care of it. All beings in the six realms, however various their joys and sorrows, are in exactly the same situation as ourselves. They are one with us in wanting to be happy and not wanting to suffer. For this very reason, just as this so-called body of ours is identified as a single entity, in exactly the same way, the whole aggregate of sentient beings could and should be identified as "I," our "I." We should protect them from suffering in just the same way as we protect ourselves.

Suppose we were to ask someone how many bodies he had. "What are you talking about?" he would say. "I have nothing but this one body!" "Well," we continue, "are there many bodies that you have to take care of?" "No indeed!" would be the reply. "I take care only of this one body of mine." But whatever he may say, the fact is that "his body" is merely a name applied to a collection of elements. Other than that, there is no such thing as an individual entity called "his body." Furthermore, there are no grounds for insisting that the term *body* should be applied here and not elsewhere. The name *body* is affixed, without ultimate justification, to what is merely a heap of component items, and it is only mentally that an idea of "my body" arises. On this basis, "I," "mine," and all the rest are imputed. To claim, moreover, that it is reasonable to apply "I" to "this aggregate," and not to apply "I" to "another aggregate," is quite unfounded. Consequently, the teachings affirm that by applying the name *I* to the whole collection of suffering beings, and by entertaining and habituating oneself to the thought *"They are myself,"* the thought of "I" will in fact arise with regard to them, and one will come to care for them as much as one now cares for oneself.

But how can such an attitude arise, given that others do not feel my pains, and I do not feel theirs? The sense of the root text (verses 92 and 93) may be construed as follows:

> Even if these sufferings of mine have no effect upon the bodies of other sentient beings, they are nevertheless the sufferings of my "I"; they are hard for me to bear precisely because of my ego identity. Again, even if the pains of others do not actually befall me, since I am a bodhisattva and consider others as myself, they are in fact my sufferings and so are unbearable.

How is it that when suffering befalls us, the pain affects only ourselves, leaving others untouched? The reason is that (in each successive incarnation) from beginningless time until the present, our minds enter amid the generative substances of our parents as they come together. Subsequently, our bodies come into being and are identified as "I"— ourselves—so that when pain occurs (in our bodies), *we* find it unbearable. And yet, from the standpoint of suffering *as such,* the distinction between *"others'* suffering" and *"my* suffering" is quite unreal. It follows that, even if the pain of another does not actually afflict me, nevertheless, if that other is identified as "I" or "mine," the suffering of that other becomes unbearable to me also. Maitriyogin, the disciple of the Lord Atīsha, did indeed feel the suffering of other beings as his own.[132] This was the experience of one who had attained the bodhisattva grounds. However, even on the level of ordinary people, we can take the example of a mother who would rather die than that her little baby should fall sick. Because she identifies with her baby, the child's suffering is actually unbearable for her. Other people who do not identify with the child are for this reason unaffected by its pain. If they did so, the child's suffering would be intolerable for them as well.

Moreover, a long period of habituation is not necessary for this kind of experience to occur. Take the example of a horse that is being put up for sale. Right up to the moment when the deal is struck, if the horse lacks grass or water, or if it is ill, or if it has any other discomfort—all this will be unbearable to its owner, while it will not at all affect the client. As soon as the transaction takes place, however, it is the buyer who will not be able to stand the horse's sufferings, while the seller will cease to be concerned. From the horse's side, of course, there are no grounds for distinction between "seller's horse" and "buyer's horse." The horse is identified simply according to how it is labeled—now as this man's horse and now as that man's horse.

In exactly the same way, there is not the slightest reason for saying that the notion of "I" must be applied to me and not to another. As we have said, "I" and "other" are merely conceptual imputations. The "I" of oneself is "other" for someone else, while what is "other" to oneself is "I" for another. The notions of "here" and "there" are simply points of view, imputed by the mind; there is no such thing as an absolute "here" or an absolute "there." In just the same way, there is no "I" and no "other" in an absolute sense. And so the Dharma teaches that it is through understanding this crucial point of mental imputation that "I" can be mentally applied to other sentient beings. If one can mentally incorporate others into the notion of "I"—the thought that they are "mine" will arise.

This is how buddhas and bodhisattvas claim sentient beings as their own selves in the way explained above, so that even the slightest pain of others is for them as if their entire body were on fire. Neither have they the slightest hesitation in doing so, just as when Devadatta shot down the swan and the Buddha claimed the bird as his.[133] In just the same way, Machig[134] said that in the centuries after her, perverted practitioners of *chöd* would with violent means subjugate the wealth-gods, ghosts, and demons, whom she had taken with the crook of her compassion—meaning by this that she had taken such gods and spirits to herself as beings whom she cherished.

As we have said, taking sentient beings as one's own does not require lengthy training. For example, if you tell someone that you will give him an old horse, no sooner are the words out of your mouth than the other person has already appropriated the horse as his property and cannot bear it if the horse is in distress. Still it might be thought that, because one has drifted into such bad mental habits, the thought of taking others as oneself will never arise. But Lord Buddha has said that in all the world, he never saw anything easier to educate than the mind itself, once it is set on the right path and steps are taken to subjugate it. On the other hand, he also said that there is nothing harder to govern than an untrained mind. Therefore, if we do not let our minds stray on to wrong paths but train them, it is perfectly possible to bring them into submission. Again, if our minds are not subdued, it is impossible for us to overcome anything else. And so the teachings say that we should strive to subdue our minds.

Common sense shows that it is necessary to be rid of suffering. And so, Shāntideva resolves [94] to clear away all the ultimately futile suffering of sentient beings, for the simple reason that it is suffering—no different, as he appropriately remarks, from his own sufferings of hunger, thirst, and so forth. And he goes on to say that he will benefit other beings and make them happy, for the simple reason that they are beings, no different from himself. [95] After all, since there is not the slightest difference between himself and others—in that all want to be happy—what reason does he have for securing happiness for himself alone? [96] And again, given that there is not the slightest difference between himself and others—in that all want to escape from pain—what reason is there, Shāntideva asks, for protecting only himself from it and not others also?

[97] Of course, someone could object, saying, "Yes, I am afflicted by my own sufferings and therefore have to prevent it. On the other hand, when suffering occurs to others, it does not touch me and therefore there is nothing for me to protect myself from." But major sufferings, for example those of an infernal existence in a future life, and also the pains of tomorrow or next month, as well as the subtler pains that arise from one moment to the next, through lack of food and clothing and so on—all these sufferings, whether great or small, are located in the future. They are not actually harming me in the present instant. If,

Shāntideva asks, these pains of the future are not tormenting me now in the present, what do I have to protect myself from? It is illogical to claim that there is something. But of course it will be said that my future suffering is different from the suffering of others. [98] For even if my future pains are not actually affecting me now, I will indeed have to undergo them later on; that is why I must prevent them. However, to cling, on the gross level, to the aggregates of this life and the next life as constituting a single entity, and to cling, on the subtler level, to the aggregates of one instant and the next as being the same thing, is a mistaken conception, nothing more. With regard to this life and the next, the entity that dies and passes out of life is not the same as that which is born in the succeeding existence, and conversely that which takes birth in the next life, wherever that may be, is not the same as that which has perished in the previous existence.

The length of time spent in the human world is the result of past karma. When this is exhausted, as the final moment of the human consciousness ends, it creates the immediate cause (of the new life), while the karma that brings about birth in a hell realm, or whatever, constitutes the cooperative cause. Wherever a person is born afterward, whether in the hells or elsewhere, at death he has a human body, whereas at birth, he has the body of a hell being and so forth. In the same way, the previous consciousness now terminated is that of a human, while at the moment of the later birth, the consciousness is that of a hell being. The two are thus distinct. In other words, when the mind and the body of the human come to an end, the mind and body of the following life come into being. It is not that there is a transmigration of something from a former to a subsequent state. As it is said:

> Readings, mirrors, lamps, and seals,
> Lenses, seeds, and tastes and sounds:
> The aggregates are thus, at times of birth and death.
> There is no transmigration, this the wise should know.

When, for example, one uses a lamp to light another lamp, the later flame cannot be lit without dependence on the first; but at the same time, the first flame does not pass into the later one.

If the earlier entity is terminated, however, and the later one arises in such a way that the two are quite separate, it will be objected that in that case the effect of former karma is necessarily lost, while (in the course of the subsequent existence) karmic effects will be encountered that have not been accumulated. But this is not so. Phenomenal appearances arise ineluctably *through the interdependence of causes and conditions.* And these same appearances cannot withstand analysis,[135] with the result that they cannot be said to be produced, or not to be produced. This, together with the assertion that karmic effects are not wasted or lost, is the specific position of the Buddhist teaching. However, the truth of this is seen fully only by one who has attained the omniscient state. It is thus to be accepted through reliance on the word of the Conqueror.

As it is said:[136]

What arises in dependence on another,
Is not at all that thing itself—
But neither is it something different:
It neither is nor is it not.

Apart from imputation, there is neither identity nor difference.[137] Accordingly, the manifesting consciousness appears as this or that according to karma, whether good or bad. But in itself, it is moments of mere knowing, clear and cognizant, arising uninterruptedly in like sequence.[138] It transcends assertions of existence or nonexistence. Thus the results of karma are not lost, and one never encounters karmic effects that have not been accumulated.

And if one considers the subtler level of temporal instants, all things in the outer or inner sphere are momentary, passing through a sequence of points in time. The earlier moment ceases and the subsequent one supervenes so that the one is distinct from the other. Likewise, when the karma for remaining in the human state provides the circumstances, and the final moment of consciousness provides the cause, the following moment of consciousness comes to birth and arises in like sequence. But the two moments are separate.

APPENDIX 3

Exchanging Self and Other

The following passage, also taken from the commentary of Kunzang Palden, is an explanation of exchanging self and other, a practice unique to the Bodhicharyāvatāra. It explains how one can, by a feat of sympathetic imagination, place oneself in the position of others. In so doing, one gains an appreciation of both how and why others feel the way they do, and how one appears in their eyes.

THE EXCHANGE OF SELF AND OTHER

When you perform the meditation of exchange, take other sentient beings who are your inferiors, superiors, or equals and consider them as yourself, putting yourself in their position. Simply take their place and entertain no other thought. Imagine yourself in the position of someone lower than yourself and develop a sense of envy [i.e., toward yourself]. Consider yourself from the viewpoint of someone on a par with yourself and generate an attitude of rivalry and competitiveness. Finally, look at yourself from the viewpoint of someone higher than yourself and cultivate feelings of pride and condescension.

THE PRACTICE OF ENVY FROM THE POINT OF VIEW OF AN INFERIOR (VERSES 141–146)

In each of these three meditations, whenever the text says "he," the reference is to our [real] "I," now regarded as "other," someone else.

And when the text says "I," it is referring to the other—high, low, or equal, as the case may be—with whom we have now identified. We should gradually cultivate the antidotes to pride, rivalry, and jealousy. The reason for this is that these three defilements arise as soon as even the slightest virtue appears in the mind stream. They are like demons that sap our integrity; and this is why the importance of antidotes is stressed in the Teachings.

Now, of the eight worldly dharmas, honor, possessions, adulation, and happiness are all productive of pride. So place yourself, for example, in the position of a beggar or tramp, someone contemptible, the dregs of society. Perform the exchange, imagining that you are that poor person. Now develop a sense of envy. [141] Looking up at yourself, your ego, now regarded as someone else, someone talented, consider how happy he must be, praised by all and sundry. You, on the other hand, are nothing, nobody, a complete down-and-out. You are utterly miserable. The other person is rich, with plenty to eat, clothes to wear, money to spend—while you have nothing. The other person is praised for his learning and ability; he's looked up to as someone worthy of reverence. You, on the other hand, are dismissed as a fool. While he enjoys a wealth of every comfort and happiness, you by contrast are a pauper, your mind burdened with anxiety, your body racked with disease, suffering the discomforts of heat and cold. [142] You have to labor like a slave, digging and gathering roots, while he can sit back with nothing to do. As these thoughts pass through your mind, feel your envy. He, your ego, even has servants and his own private horse, on whom he inflicts a great deal of discomfort and suffering. He is not even aware that they are in distress; and there he is, oh so comfortable. And as if that weren't enough, he gets angry and lashes out, whipping and beating them. Put yourself in the position of his poor victims and take their suffering on yourself. If you do, the teachings say that you will come to recognize their sorrows. Compassion for them will grow, with the result that you will not harm them anymore.

Once again, reflect that he, your ego, is talented and of good family, wealthy and surrounded by friends. You, on the other hand, are a complete nonentity with a reputation for being totally untalented. [143] But, even though you have nothing to show for yourself, you might well ask *him* what reason he has to be so arrogant. After all, the existence or nonexistence of qualities and the concepts of high and low are all relative. There are no absolute values. Even people who are low down like you can be seen to have some good qualities, relatively speaking, while, compared with someone with extremely great talents, he (your ego) is inferior. On the other hand, compared with a person extremely disfavored, feeble with age, lame or blind, and so on, you are much better off. After all, you are able to walk on your own two feet, you can see with your eyes, and you are not crippled with age. You have at least something.

Furthermore, the stanza beginning "What! A nobody without distinction" may be understood in a different sense, namely that you have it in you to acquire all the excellence of training, since you have all qualities of the pure tathāgatagarbha, the seed of buddhahood, implicit in your nature. Thus you are far from being bereft of good qualities.

[144] If your haughty ego retorts that you are despicable because your discipline and understanding are poor, or that you lack means and so forth, this is not because in yourself you are evil, or that you are just inept; it is because your afflictions of desire, ignorance, avarice, and so on are so powerful that you are helpless. And so you should answer him saying: "All right, if you really are a qualified bodhisattva, you should help me as much as you can, and to the extent that my discipline, view, and ability are poor. And since my reformation, the purification of my discipline and understanding, and the acquisition of great abilities would be of great benefit to me, I am even prepared to accept punishment from you—harsh words and beating—just like a schoolboy learning his letters has to take beatings from his tutor. [145] But the fact is that you, the great bodhisattva, are doing nothing for me; you don't even give me a scrap of food or something to drink. So why are you passing yourself off as someone worthy? You have no right to look down on me and behave scornfully toward me and my likes. And in any case, even if you had real virtues, if you can't give me any relief or help, what use are your qualities to me? They are totally irrelevant. What is more, if you have the qualities of a bodhisattva but lack compassion, [146] if you can stand by without the slightest intention of helping and saving me and those like me, who through the power of our evil karma are on our way to the lower realms,

as though falling into the mouth of a ferocious beast—you are guilty of a great and unspeakable sin! And all the time there you are, passing yourself off as someone wonderful, while the fact is that you have no good qualities at all. You put yourself on a level with the real bodhisattvas, the skilled ones who in their compassion really do take up the burdens of others. Your behavior is completely outrageous!"

This is how to meditate on envy and resentment as the chief antidote to pride. By appreciating the suffering involved in being a lowly person, without talents or honor, we come to realize how wrong it is to be arrogant and scornful. It dawns on us how unpleasant it is for someone in a humble position when we are proud and supercilious toward them. We should stop behaving like this and begin to treat people with respect, providing them with sustenance and clothing and striving to give them practical help.

THE PRACTICE OF JEALOUS RIVALRY FROM THE POINT OF VIEW OF AN EQUAL (VERSES 147–150)

In order to generate a sense of competitiveness, take someone similar to, or slightly better than, yourself in religious or worldly affairs. [147] Make the exchange, taking the other person's place. Tell yourself that however good his reputation is, you will outdo him (i.e., your ego). Whatever possessions he has, and whatever respect he has in other people's eyes, you will rob him of them in contests or debates, and you will most certainly get them for yourself. [148] In every way possible, you will advertise far and wide your own spiritual and material gifts, while hushing up whatever talents he has, so that no one will ever see them or hear about them. [149] By contrast, you will dissimulate whatever faults you have, hiding them from the public gaze, while at the same time talking about all his shortcomings, making quite sure that they are known to everyone. Under the impression that you are beyond reproach, lots of people will congratulate you, while for him it will be just the opposite. From now on, you will be the wealthy one, the center of attention. For him, there will be nothing. [150] For a long time and with intense satisfaction, you will gloat over the penalties he has to suffer for breaking his vows of religion, or because he has misbehaved in worldly life. You will make him an object of scorn and derision, and in public gatherings you will make him despicable in people's eyes, digging out and exposing all his secret sins.

Thus by using a spirit of rivalry as an antidote to jealousy, you will recognize your own faults in being competitive with others. Then you should discontinue such an evil attitude, and instead do whatever you can to help your rivals with presents and honors.

 ### The Practice of Pride from the Point of View of a Superior (Verses 151–154)

Imagine yourself in the position of someone superior, who looks down on you with pride and derision, and thinks like this: [151] Reflect that you have heard that this person (your ego), this nonentity, is trying to put himself on a par with you. But how, everyone is asking, could anyone even make a comparison between him and you—in learning, intelligence, good looks, social class, wealth, and possessions? The whole idea is absurd; it is like comparing the earth with the sky! [152] Hearing everyone talk about your talents, about all your learning and so on, saying how it sets you apart from such an abject individual, is extremely gratifying. Indeed, the thrill of it is so intense that your flesh stands up in goose pimples. Savor the feeling! Really enjoy it!

[153] If through his labors, and despite the obstacles you throw in his way, he manages to make some progress, you agree that, so long as he abases himself and respectfully follows your instructions, this low-down wretch will get the merest necessities in return: food to fill his stomach and enough clothes on his back to keep out the wind. But as for anything extra, you, being the stronger, will snatch it away and deprive him of it. [154] Every kind of pleasure this inferior might have, you will undermine, and more than that, you will constantly attack him, piling on all kinds of opprobrium.

But why are you being so vicious? Because of all the many hundreds of times that this person (this ego of yours) has harmed you while you were wandering in saṃsāra. In other words, as you decide that you will constantly try to damage and wear away the satisfaction of this self-cherishing mentality, and as you tell yourself that it is precisely this self-centered attitude that has brought you suffering so many hundreds of times in the hells and other places of saṃsāra, the fault of *not* being rid of pride will become evident.

Therefore, use this meditation on pride as the principal antidote to jealous resentment. When someone superior to you behaves proudly and insults you with his overweening attitude, you will think to yourself, "Why is this person being so arrogant and offensive?" But instead of being envious and resentful, change places. Using the meditation on pride, place yourself in that position of superiority, and ask yourself whether you have the same feelings of pride and condescension. If you perceive the way in which you too have sentiments of pride, scorn, and contempt to those lower down than yourself, you will be able to look at the person being arrogant to you and think, "Well, yes, I quite understand why he feels the way he does." And so you should serve him respectfully, avoiding attitudes of rivalry and contention.

NOTES

1. There are two Sanskrit titles of Shāntideva's work. The longer one, *Bodhisattvacharyāvatāra*, was rendered literally as the title of the Tibetan version (*spyang chub sems dpa'i spyod pa la 'jug pa*), the literal meaning of which is "The Entrance to the Way of the Bodhisattva." There exists a shorter and much-used title, *Bodhicharyāvatāra*, which means "Entrance to the Path of Awakening."

2. See Appendix 1 for a traditional account of Shāntideva's life. Additional details may be found in the excellent introductions to the translation of the *Bodhicharyāvatāra* by Kate Crosby and Andrew Skilton (Oxford University Press, 1996).

3. See verses 23–24 of chapter 3.

4. See also H. H. Dalai Lama, *Path to Bliss* (Snow Lion, 1991), pp. 161–174.

5. This account of Mādhyamika is heavily dependent on T. R. V. Murti's remarkable book *The Central Philosophy of Buddhism*, which is warmly recommended to the interested reader.

6. The *Majjhima Nikāya* is a section of the Pāli Scriptures.

7. *Saṃyutta Nikāya*, II.

8. See Nāgārjuna, *Mūlamādhyamikakārikā* (Tib. *dbu ma rtsa ba'i shes rab*) XV, 7.

9. This in fact is the usual approach of Western orientalists of earlier generations. See, for example, Stcherbatsky, *Buddhist Nirvāṇa*, pp. 6 and 23; also

Louis Finot in the introduction to his translation of the *Bodhicharyāva-tāra, La Marche à la lumière.*

10. See Murti, chap. 2.

11. See Murti, pp. 293–301 and passim.

12. Coming after Āryadeva (c. 180–200 CE), but before Chandrakīrti (early seventh century), Buddhapālita (first half of fifth century) asserted the technique of *reductio ad absurdum* or *prasaṅga* to be the essence of Mādhyamika. This was questioned by his contemporary, Bhāvaviveka, who said that the mere negation of a theory should be supplemented with the assertion of a counter position. He was the founder of the so-called Svātantrika-Mādhyamika, with the result that the Mādhyamika was divided into two schools. Coming after him, Chandrakīrti vindicated Prāsaṅgika-Mādhyamika, the position of Buddhapālita, as the true sense of Mādhyamika, and severely criticized Bhāvaviveka. See Murti, p. 95f.; also Bhikshu Sangharakshita, *A Survey of Buddhism*, p. 346. All four schools of Tibetan Buddhism uphold Prāsaṅgika-Mādhyamika as the supreme philosophical position.

13. Rinchen Zangpo (rin chen bzang po), the first of the translators of the New Translation (gsar ma) School.

14. See Bibliography.

15. Patrul Rinpoche, Jigme Chökyi Wangpo ('jigs med chos kyi dbang po) 1808–1887, author of the celebrated *kun bzang bla mai zhal lung*, translated as *The Words of My Perfect Teacher*, translated by the Padmakara Translation Group, Sacred Literature Series (HarperCollins, 1994).

16. See biographical note in Dilgo Khyentse Rinpoche, *Heart Treasure of the Enlightened Ones*, Shambhala, 1992. See also the forthcoming biography of Patrul Rinpoche, translated by the Padmakara Translation Group.

17. "Those who go in bliss" (Tib. bde gshegs; Skt. sugata): a title of the buddhas.

18. The word Dharma is here a translation of the Tibetan *chos sku* (Skt. *dharmakāya*), literally the "Dharma body." According to the commentarial tradition, two interpretations are possible. The term may be taken to mean simply "the body of the teachings" (which is the interpretation of Khenpo Kunpel and Khenpo Shenga), with the result that the first line of the poem consists of a salutation to the Three Jewels of Buddha, Dharma, and Saṅgha. On the other hand, it may be understood as referring to the dharmakāya or "truth body," the absolute aspect of a buddha, i.e., one of

the three bodies of a buddha, along with the sambhogakāya or "body of divine enjoyment," and the nirmāṇakāya or "body of manifestation."

19. The heirs of the buddhas are the bodhisattvas, those who aim to attain buddhahood for the sake of all beings. In this context, reference is actually being made to superior bodhisattvas, whose realization corresponds to the Mahāyāna path of seeing and beyond, in other words who are abiding on the bodhisattva bhūmis or grounds, and who are therefore sublime objects of refuge.

20. In order to progress toward enlightenment, it is necessary to possess eight forms of ease, or freedom, and ten forms of wealth. The former are: the freedom of not being born (1) in one of the hells, (2) as a preta or hungry ghost, (3) as an animal, (4) in the realms of the gods of measureless lifespan, (5) among barbarians who are ignorant of the teachings and practices of the Buddhadharma, (6) as one with wrong views concerning karma and so forth, (7) in a time and place where a buddha has not appeared, and (8) as mentally and physically handicapped.
The ten forms of wealth or endowment are subdivided into five considered as intrinsic and five as extrinsic to the personality. The five intrinsic endowments are (1) to be born a human being, (2) to inhabit a "central land," i.e., where the Dharma is proclaimed, (3) to be in possession of normal faculties, (4) to be one who is not karmically inclined to great negativity, and (5) to have faith in the Dharma. The five extrinsic endowments are the facts that (1) a buddha has appeared in the universe in which one is living, and at an accessible time, (2) that he has expounded the Doctrine, (3) that his Doctrine still persists, (4) that it is practiced, and (5) that one has been accepted by a spiritual master.

21. The Tibetan word *chu shing* ("water tree") denotes a hollow plant that dies after bearing fruit. Often, when the latter characteristic is being emphasized, the word is translated "plantain," but when its hollowness is in question, the term is sometimes, as elsewhere in the present text, rendered as "banana tree."

22. The reference is to Maitreya, the Buddha of the future, as recounted in the *Gaṇḍavyūha-sūtra.*

23. Tathāgata (Tib. de bzhin gshegs pa): literally "one thus gone," a title of the Buddha.

24. A reference to the *Subāhu-paripricchā-sūtra,* the *Sūtra of the Questions of Subāhu.* The Sanskrit original of this sūtra has been lost, but is preserved in a Chinese translation.

25. According to ancient Indian tradition, the ṛishis were sages who perceived the sound of the Vedas and transmitted them to the world. They form a class by themselves between gods and humans.

26. Brahmā, the creator of the universe according to the Vedas.

27. The actual confession, from which this chapter takes its name, begins at verse 27. It is preceded by the traditional formulas of homage and offering.

28. Samantabhadra is the bodhisattva associated with prayer and unlimited offerings; Mañjughoṣha (also known as Mañjushrī) is the bodhisattva personifying wisdom; Lokeshvara ("Lord of the World"), otherwise known as Avalokiteshvara (Tib. spyan ras gzigs), is the bodhisattva of compassion.

29. The expression "jewels of Dharma" refers to the sacred texts. These are divided into twelve categories: (1) sūtra (Tib. mdo sde), condensed discourses covering a single topic; (2) geya (Tib. dbyangs bsnyad), poetic epitome (of more detailed teachings in prose); (3) vyākaraṇa (Tib. lung bstan), prophecies; (4) gāthā (Tib. tshigs bcad), discourses in verse; (5) udāna (Tib. ched du brjod pa), instructions given by the Buddha spontaneously in order to maintain the Dharma; (6) nidāna (Tib. gleng gzhi), instructions following specific incidents (e.g., the rules of Vinaya); (7) avadāna (Tib. rtogs brjod), life stories concerning contemporaries of the Buddha; (8) itivṛittaka (Tib. de lta bu byung ba), historical accounts; (9) jātaka (Tib. skyes rabs), previous lives of the Buddha when he was a bodhisattva; (10) vaipulya (Tib. shin tu rgyas pa), long, complex explanations; (11) adbhūtadharma (Tib. rmad byung), extraordinary teachings; (12) upadesha (Tib. gtan dbab), instructions on specific topics (clarifying the sense of the Vinaya and Sūtra: classification of saṃsāric phenomena—aggregates, elements, āyatanas; outline of the phenomena of the path—grounds, paths, concentrations; enumeration of resultant phenomena—kāyas and wisdoms; and so on).

30. In the traditional practice of prostration, it is normal to imagine that one possesses innumerable bodies, all prostrating at the same time.

31. This is a formula for the taking of refuge whereby one enters the door of the Dharma and becomes a follower of the Buddha.

32. Yama, the King of Death—not a sentient being so much as a personification and symbol.

33. Ākāshagarbha and Kṣhitigarbha are two of the eight major bodhisattvas known as the eight close sons (i.e., of the Buddha).

34. Vajrapāṇi is also one of the eight close sons. He is one of the three bodhisattvas (the others being Mañjushrī and Avalokiteshvara) known as the

Protectors of the Three Lineages. Vajrapāṇi is the embodiment of the power of all the buddhas.

35. The happiness or suffering of postmortem states can arise only as the fruit of past actions. At the moment of death, we are helped or harmed only by the merits or evils contained in our own mind streams. We can be neither assisted nor harmed through the actions of others. By what criteria, then, are we to distinguish, at the moment of death, between friend and foe?

36. There are two kinds of negative actions: those that are evil by their nature and those that are evil because they contravene an injunction or violate a promise or vow. The former category comprises the ten nonvirtuous actions: killing, stealing, sexual misconduct, lying, divisive speech, harsh speech, idle chatter, covetousness, harmful intent, and false views. The second category would include, for example, the contravening of a religious commitment, thus separating the practitioner from progress on the path.

37. See note 44.

38. See note 19. According to the standard teaching, there are ten bodhisattva grounds or stages, extending from entry to the Mahāyāna path of seeing, throughout the path of meditation, and until attainment of the path of no more learning, which is buddhahood. Note: this two-line verse does not appear in the extant Sanskrit version.

39. The reference here is to seven traditional actions of accumulating merit (very often expressed in verse formulas). These are: prostration, offering, confession, rejoicing in all good actions, the request for teachings, the request for the teachers to remain in the world and not to pass into nirvāṇa, and dedication. The first three actions formed the content of the previous chapter; the remaining four are expressed here in the opening stanzas of chap. 3.

40. A reference to the *antarakalpa*, the period of extreme decadence, figuring in the ancient Indian conception of temporal sequences, in which the quality of human life gradually declines until the age of ten years marks the summit of growth and capacity. It is a time marked by extreme instability and famine.

41. The celebrated case of this was that of the Buddha's disciple Shāriputra, as recorded in the *Saddharma-puṇḍarīka-sūtra* (Tib. *dam pa'i chos pad ma dkar po*). It is said that Shāriputra was a practitioner of the Mahāyāna who had progressed far along the path. One day a demon appeared to

him and, wishing to put him to the test and if possible contrive his downfall, asked him for his right hand. In reply, Shāriputra cut it off and gave
it to the demon. But the demon was angry and refused to accept it, com-
plaining that Shāriputra had impolitely offered it to him with his left! At
this point, it is said that Shāriputra lost hope of ever being able to satisfy
the desires of beings, and turned from the Mahāyāna to pursue the path
to arhatship.

42. The ability to perceive a buddha and to benefit from the teachings of such
a being requires the correct karmic disposition and implies the presence
of a considerable degree of merit in the mind stream of the disciple. The
fact that one has not been liberated through the teachings of the buddhas
of the past serves to underline the importance of the present moment,
when one has encountered the Dharma, and throws into relief the great
significance of a relationship with an accomplished spiritual master.

43. According to Buddhist teachings (see remarks in the Introduction), karmic results follow ineluctably upon the perpetration of acts, irrespective
of conscious attitude or moral conscience (although the quality and force
of the act may be significantly affected thereby). Thus beings in the lower
states, animals for example, do indeed accumulate karma and must
sooner or later experience the consequences of their actions, even though
these may be performed under the irresistible influence of instinct. And
the karmic situation is compounded, rather than mitigated, by an uncon-
sciousness of the Dharma. The strength of instinctual habit and the ignorance of what behavior is to be adopted and what behavior is to be
abandoned constitutes one of the principal miseries of existence in states
other than that of the precious human condition.

44. According to the Buddhist teachings, the experience of beings in saṃsāra
falls into six broad categories, states, or realms. Birth in these worlds is
the fruit of past karma or action. There are three unfortunate states in
which suffering predominates over every other experience: that of animals, hungry ghosts, and beings in the hells. There are three fortunate
realms (the happy states referred to in this verse), where suffering is mitigated by temporal pleasures, namely: the heavens of the mundane gods,
the realms of the asuras or demigods, and the human condition. The
misery of beings in the lower realms, sometimes called the states of loss,
is compounded by the fact that their ability to create the positive energy
necessary to propel them into higher existences is very weak, while negativity abounds. For this reason, beings in the lower realms rarely emerge
and tend to sink deeper and deeper.

45. Mount Meru, the axis of the universe according to traditional Hindu-
Buddhist cosmology.

46. The point being made is that pledges should be honored. In order to liberate others it is necessary to be free oneself, and Shāntideva is saying that the purification of one's own defilements is the best way of helping others. It is the indispensable first step.

47. As a spur for the practice of pure ethics, and as an object for meditation on compassion, the Buddhist teachings describe the various experiences of the hell realms in considerable detail. The torments that beings undergo there, as well as the topography of the hells themselves, are, as in any other realm of saṃsāra, ultimately unreal—the hallucinatory, dreamlike result of actions committed in the past. The karmic fruit of sexual miscon- duct is the situation in which the person finds himself upon the infernal hill of shālmali trees. There he sees a vision of the former object of his passion. Climbing the hill, cutting himself all the while on the razor-sharp leaves of the trees, he finds that his former lover turns into a horrific demoness who begins to devour him. See Patrul Rinpoche's *The Words of My Perfect Teacher* for a vivid description of this encounter.

48. The triple world comprises the three worlds of saṃsāra: the desire realm (kāmadhātu), the form realm (rūpadhātu), and the realm of formlessness (ārūpadhātu). The desire realm consists of the six states of saṃsāra from the hells up to and including the six levels of the desire realm gods. The form and formless realms are celestial existences superior to those in- cluded in the desire realm.

49. Cliffs and mountains in hell that repeatedly rush together and overwhelm the beings caught between them. See Patrul Rinpoche's *The Words of My Perfect Teacher.*

50. For example, meditation on patience as an antidote to anger, or on the disgusting aspects of the body as an antidote to desire.

51. The expression "field of qualities" refers to the buddhas and bodhisattvas; the "field of benefits" refers to all those who bring benefits—parents, friends, and so on; the "field of sorrow" (usually termed the "field of compassion") refers to all other beings who suffer or who are in some way disadvantaged, e.g., the sick, way-worn travelers, and others.

52. The six perfections (Skt. pāramitā) form the essential practice of the Mahāyāna. They are generosity, ethical discipline, patience, joyous effort, concentration, and wisdom.

53. According to Mahāyāna teaching, in extreme circumstances and when the motives are exclusively those of compassion, actions of body and speech

normally proscribed in the list of the ten nonvirtues (see note 36) may be performed.

54. In other words, the doctrine of the Mahāyāna—"vast" in activities and skillful means, and "deep" in the wisdom of emptiness.

55. A reference to those following the Shrāvakayāna and Mahāyāna teachings, respectively.

56. Making the person believe, for example, that tantric practice is alone worthwhile, and giving to understand that study and the rules of ethical discipline may be neglected.

57. According to the literal precepts of the Vinaya discipline (originally conceived within the context of traditional Indian society), it is an infraction for monks to be alone with women unrelated by family ties.

58. In India and Tibet, contrary to the West, the snapping of the fingers is considered a polite way of attracting attention.

59. *The Sūtra in Three Sections* (Skt. *Triskandha-sūtra*) consists of confession before the thirty-five buddhas, verses in praise of virtue, and a dedication of merits.

60. The Mahāyāna, or "Great Vehicle," is the path of the bodhisattvas. It consists of the practice of universal compassion and the cultivation of the wisdom of emptiness, the ultimate nature of self and of all phenomena. Based on the motivation and wish to deliver all beings without exception from the sufferings of the unenlightened state, it leads to the attainment of buddhahood for the sake of others. The Mahāyāna is the form of Buddhism that flourished in the northern countries of Asia: China, Korea, Japan, Mongolia, and Tibet.

61. *The Biography of the Glorious Sambhava* (Skt. *Shrīsambhava-vimokṣha*) is in fact a chapter in the *Gaṇḍavyūha-sūtra*, in which the following passage is to be found:

> If you would pay due homage to the spiritual master, let your mind be like the earth, never tiring of the burden of supporting everything; like a diamond, indestructible in its intent; like a rampart, wherein suffering can find no breach; like a slave, never jibbing at all that must be done; like a faithful beast of burden, never restive; like a ferry boat, always willing to go back and forth; and like a perfect son who drinks in with his eyes the countenance of his spiritual father.
> O noble child, look upon yourself as a sick man, your

spiritual master as a physician, his teachings as a healing draft, and your sincere practice as the path to health.

62. *The Sūtra of the Essence of the Sky* (Skt. *Ākāshagarbha-sūtra*).

63. *The Digest of All Disciplines* (Skt. *Shikṣhāsamuchchaya*, Tib. *bslab btus*); *the Digest of the Sūtras* (Skt. *Sūtrasamuchchaya*, Tib. *mdo btus*): see remarks in the Introduction.

64. A reference to devotees of the Hindu goddess Durgā, whose cult demanded the practice of extreme austerities.

65. In the next nine rather difficult verses, Shāntideva discusses and undermines the ordinary common sense attitude to enemies and other irritants. The argument proceeds as follows. First, in stanzas 22–26, Shāntideva affirms that there is no such thing as an independent agent, i.e., acting in the absence of conditioning factors. Usually it is thought reasonable to resent the hostile behavior of another being, while it is generally recognized that anger against an inanimate object is futile and somehow irrational, since the object in question only harms us under the influence of other forces. But Shāntideva argues that this is equally true of animate sources of our suffering. They, too, are impelled by the extrinsic factors of negative emotion. It is as irrational to hate a human aggressor, victim in turn of his own defilements, as it is to hate a tree that has been blown over by the wind and has flattened our car. Anger against an enemy cannot be justified, says Shāntideva, because ultimately the enemy is not "himself" to blame. The point is repeated in stanza 41.

Of course, there is an obvious objection to this. Even admitting the power of emotion, it seems wrong to place animate and inanimate entities in the same category. A human aggressor, unlike a tree, is after all an accountable agent; and a person's actions cannot be defined simply in terms of other factors—as a mere interplay of impersonal forces. According to this line of reasoning, there must surely exist a proper object of resentment, namely the aggressor "himself"—or, to put it another way, the "self" of the aggressor.

This raises a specifically metaphysical question, and even though much greater attention is paid to it in the course of the ninth chapter, Shāntideva is obliged here to focus briefly (stanzas 27–30) on the ideas of "primal substance" (pradhāna) and the "self" (atmān), as upheld variously by the different schools of non-Buddhist Indian philosophy. For all these schools, it was axiomatic that the self and the primal substance were (1) independent entities and (2) permanent or immutable. But Shāntideva points out that if there were a such a thing as an independent, permanent self, temporary emotional states, such as hostility, could never be said to arise in it without denying the self's permanence. "That which was not hostile" and "that which is now hostile" are not the same entity. Consequently, if the self is unchanging, it can never premeditate and actualize hostility (27.3–4 and 28.1–2) and thus cannot be held responsible for an act of aggression. In other words, a theory of the self can never rationally justify resentment and retaliation against an aggressor. However abstruse these arguments may seem, it should be noted that their purpose is entirely practical. The knowledge that an attacker is driven by other forces, and is not *in himself* an enemy, is a powerful aid in controlling and eliminating one's own aggressive response.

66. Lines 3 and 4 of stanza 28 are a brief reference to the Sāṃkhya theory of Puruṣha and Prākṛiti. If the self is permanent and immutable, it follows that its apprehension of an object must be permanent also. A succession of different perceptions is impossible. Thus the self of another being cannot *become* hostile toward us. If it is hostile now, it must have always been so and will remain so permanently—which is absurd. It should be noted here, as elsewhere, that the term "permanent" is a translation of the Tibetan word *rtag pa*. This does not mean "permanent" in the sense of being eternally existent, but only in the sense of being immutable. In fact, *rtag pa* may be applied to something that comes into and passes out of existence. It means simply that while the entity exists, it remains completely static and unchanging. According to Buddhist teaching, of course, there are no phenomena to which this term can be properly applied.

67. Stanzas 29 and 30 refer to the Nyāya-Vaisheṣhika school. According to this theory, and in contrast with that of the Sāṃkhya school and the Vedānta after it, the (permanent) Self—as distinct from the mind—is regarded as knowable. In other words, it is an object, rather than the subject, of consciousness. It is believed to enter into relation with the mind and so forth, and subsequently identify experiences as its own. Here again, belief in the permanence of the Self entails insuperable difficulties. If the Self is permanent, how could it ever be said to meet with new experiences and assimilate them? In holding that the Self is conscious or unconscious, respectively, the Sāṃkhya and Nyāya-Vaisheṣhika schools occupy, from the Mādhyamika point of view, two extremes of the metaphysical spectrum. When these two are refuted, all intermediary positions are disposed of at the same time. This is doubtless why Shāntideva juxtaposes the two theories here, as he does later in the ninth chapter.

68. See note 47.

69. The argument here is that if we are reluctant to give happiness to others, wanting rather to keep it all for ourselves, we might as well refuse to pay

the people we employ and so on, since they would be made happy by receiving their wages. But it is obvious who would be the real loser.

70. In other words, for Shāntideva, a monk, the enjoyment of honors and reputation is as inappropriate as gambling and drink.

71. Stanzas 95 and 96 should be taken together. We all like to be surrounded by admirers. But the actual pleasure that other people take in us exists only in their minds and is not transferable to ours. Even if I am the center of attention, the delight the bystanders feel is not something I am able to experience. If the simple fact of pleasure arising in the mind of someone else can give me gratification, it follows that whenever someone— anyone—is happy, I should be pleased. The fact that this is not so (as when someone I do not like steps into the limelight) shows that my happiness and my relationships all ultimately revolve around my ego, with which they are all, without exception, coordinated.

72. A buddhafield (Skt. buddhakṣhetra, Tib. rgyal ba'i zhing) is a dimension or world manifested through the enlightened aspirations of a buddha or bodhisattva in conjunction with the meritorious karma of sentient beings. Those born in a buddhafield are able to progress swiftly to enlightenment.

73. Khenpo Kunpel explains this verse as follows. A person who has perfect love for others becomes an excellent object of reverence, and offerings made to such a person are productive of extremely positive karmic results. But the perfect love of the saint only comes about in relation to other beings, which in turn reveals the value and importance of the latter.

74. This remark looks forward to an idea to be developed in the course of chapter 8. See the commentarial note in Appendix 2.

75. The word translated in this chapter as "heroic perseverance" is *brtson 'grus,* a rendering of the Sanskrit *vīrya.* Usually the Tibetan term is understood as "diligence" or "endeavor," but always connotes a sense of joy and enthusiasm, features that are brought out powerfully in the course of the chapter itself. The Sanskrit term carries with it a sense of manliness and heroism, and is connected with our word "virile," as well as "virtue." The general sense is one of great courage and perseverance: fearlessness in the face of all adversity.

76. Gods are not often considered to be liable to suffering, but according to the Buddhist view, the worldly gods, though enjoying immense longevity, are not immortal and eventually die. Having used up their entire store of karmic merit in the course of their divine and indolent existence, and being possessed of powers of clairvoyance, they realize that they must now

fall into one of the lower realms of saṃsāra and foresee the horror of their destination. See *The Words of My Perfect Teacher*, p. 93, for a detailed description.

77. These practices are discussed at length in chap. 8. See also Appendixes 2 and 3.

78. Shrāvaka (Tib. nyan thos), "hearers." This is the name given to the Hīnayāna disciples of the Buddha. They aim to free themselves from saṃsāra and attain the perfect cessation of all suffering. They lack, however, the attitude of universal compassion and responsibility, which is bodhichitta. The fruit of their path is arhatship, not buddhahood.

79. It is paradoxical that one can entertain such an extraordinary intention as bodhichitta, the wish to liberate all beings, while still imprisoned in saṃsāra with a mind stream replete with the karmic causes of immense suffering to come. Shāntideva is driving home the point that the would-be bodhisattva has a primary duty and need of self-purification.

80. This is, in fact, a description of the birth of a bodhisattva in Sukhāvatī (Tib. bde ba can), the pure land of Buddha Amitābha.

81. The *Vajradhvaja-sūtra (The Diamond Banner Sūtra)* is in fact a subsection of the larger *Avataṃsaka-sūtra*. The following passage is taken from it: "When the sun shines, O Devaputra, it illuminates the entire world, regardless of the blindness of beings and the mountain shadows. In the same way, bodhisattvas appear for the liberation of beings, regardless of the obstacles that these may present."

82. In other words, one should confidently undertake the *action* of applying the antidotes; one should courageously decide not to fall under the power of the *afflictions;* and one should have self-assurance in affirming one's *ability* to abandon evil behavior and cultivate wholesome qualities.

83. Following the terms of the comparison, the crows are the faults; one's weakness is the dying serpent.

84. Here, and in the following verses, a distinction is drawn between two kinds of pride. On the one hand, there is the positive quality of confidence leading to courage and perseverance and, on the other, the negative quality of arrogance and conceit, resulting in the overweening behavior that is often the mask of weakness. Using the same term in both senses, Shāntideva plays on the word "pride" in a way that might at first be confusing. For the sake of clarity in the translation, the two kinds of pride are more pointedly distinguished.

85. This stanza does not appear in the Sanskrit text (at least in the editions used by Louis Finot and Marion L. Matics). Some commentators have, moreover, questioned the authenticity of the half-stanza 62a. It is, however, generally included.

86. Wholesome disillusion: the Tibetan term *skyo ba*, or *skyo shes*, indicates a sense of revulsion and weariness with the futile sufferings of saṃsāra.

87. In other words, the dying person will not be worried about the sorrow caused to others by his death, for the simple reason that he will have none to mourn for him. Moreover, without this complicating factor, the meditator will be free to concentrate on the yogas to be performed at the moment of death.

88. The context here and in the following stanzas is that of the complicated rituals attending a traditional Indian marriage ceremony. In brutal contrast to the delights of romantic attachment and physical love, Shāntideva forces on us an overall contemplation of the physical realities of life and death.

89. Carefully concealed, that is, in being a skull covered with muscles, sinews, and skin—soon to be revealed in the charnel ground.

90. In other words, the uterus and seminal fluid.

91. See Appendix 2.

92. Through the practice of equalizing self and other, and exchange of self and other, the bodhisattva becomes so sensitized to the sufferings of others that these are painful even to himself.

93. Supuṣhpachandra: a bodhisattva forbidden by the king Shūradatta to teach the Dharma on pain of death, but who for the sake of others disobeyed and went cheerfully to his execution. This story is found in the *Samādhirāja-sūtra*.

94. Blood: i.e., the generative substance (ovum) of the mother.

95. In the *Gaṇḍavyūha-sūtra*, Avalokiteshvara (Tib. spyan ras gzigs) says: "Let whoever stands before a crowd invoke my name three times and have no fear."

96. I.e., the way of Dharma, leading to the realization of buddhahood—not, of course, the heavens of the worldly gods.

97. Even in terms of the present life, a spirit of selfishness and an unwillingness to cooperate lead inevitably to social disorder.

98. Compare the sentiments of this and the following stanzas with stanza 12 of the same chapter. Also see Appendix 2 for a full explanation.

99. If I give the appreciation of others as the reason for the infatuated attention I give to my own body, it follows that I should be similarly attentive to the physical comfort of others, since their appreciation is equally applied to their own bodies.

100. This stanza only occurs in the Tibetan translation; there is no equivalent in any extant Sanskrit version.

101. As already stated in the Introduction, the ninth chapter of the *Bodhicharyāvatāra* is an extremely concise exposition of Mādhyamika philosophy, recapitulating its various stages of development and polemical interaction with other schools, both Buddhist and non-Buddhist. It is worth bearing in mind that on that famous occasion when Shāntideva recited his text from the lofty throne at Nālandā, he did so to a public already deeply versed in both the content and history of Mādhyamika. And his ninth chapter was no doubt intended as a brilliant and perhaps even light-hearted exposition of a highly recondite subject to a specialist audience of philosophers and academics. As it stands, the ninth chapter is scarcely comprehensible to the unassisted reader, and an extensive commentary is indispensable. Those of Khenchen Kunzang Palden and Minyak Kunzang Sönam (see Bibliography) are already available in translation, and the interested student will also derive much help from the other commentaries listed in the Bibliography. In an attempt to render the root text at least intelligible, almost all translators have resorted to the expedient of indicating in parentheses the different points of view (Sāṃkhya, Nyāya, Abhidharma, and so on) referred to as the chapter progresses. But it is doubtful whether, in the absence of an extensive commentary, these additions do any more than complicate the issue and increase the dismay of the bewildered reader. In any case, they tend to obscure the fact that the ninth chapter, like the rest of the book, is composed in seamless verse, and is in fact a fast moving, scintillating *tour de force*. With regard to the present translation, the aim has been to facilitate comprehension as much as possible, and a certain latitude of expression seemed justifiable, mainly in the way of explanatory paraphrase where possible and appropriate. The interpretation given in the commentary of Kunzang Palden has been consistently followed.

102. According to the Sanskrit commentary of Prajñākaramati, stanzas 49 to 51 have been misplaced and are not in their correct position. According to the commentary of Gyalse Thogme, they could be inserted between

verses 43 and 44. Here we have followed the positioning of Khenchen Kunzang Palden and Mipham Rinpoche.

103. Mahākāshyapa became, after the Buddha's parinirvāṇa, the leader of the Saṅgha and played an important role in the preservation of the teachings.

104. Sukhāvatī (Tib. *bde ba can*): the pure land of Buddha Amitābha. See note 80.

105. See note 47.

106. Vaitaraṇī: name of a river in hell. Mandākinī: name of a river in heaven.

107. The One Who Holds the Lotus (Skt. *Padmapāṇi,* Tib. *phyag na pad ma*): a title of the Bodhisattva Avalokiteshvara.

108. The northern continent (Skt. *Uttarakuru,* Tib. *sgra mi snyan*): the continent to the north of Mount Meru, according to traditional Buddhist cosmology. (Our world, Jambudvīpa, is the southern continent.) The northern continent is said to be a place of great harmony and prosperity.

109. Māyādevī: the mother of Buddha Shākyamuni.

110. See the commentary of Kunzang Palden: "May all the women in the world—who are lacking in physical strength, who have to suffer the pain of bearing children, and who are tormented with the thirty-two special kinds of sickness that afflict women—acquire the same advantages as those who have a male body."

111. Perfect Joy (Skt. *Pramuditā-bhūmi,* Tib. *sa rab tu dga' ba*): name of the first of the ten bodhisattva grounds or levels. See note 19.

112. Butön (bu ston), 1290–1364, an adherent of the Sakya school and a major scholar of the Tibetan Buddhist tradition. He established and systematized the Scriptural Canon.

113. Tāranātha, alias Kunga Nyingpo (kun dga' snying po), 1575–1634: a celebrated Tibetan scholar and member of the Jonangpa school.

114. Yeshe Peljor (ye shes dpal 'byor), 1704–1777?, author of *Paksam Jönzang (dpag bsam ljon bzang),* translated and edited by Shri Sarat Chandra Das with the title: *The History of the Rise, Progress and Downfall of Buddhism in India.* See Amalia Pezzali, *Śantideva, mystique bouddhiste des VIIe et VIIIe siècles.*

115. See Pezzali, pp. 27–32.

116. The accounts of Butön and Tāranātha are the most elaborate and detailed of the four cited. They do not, however, agree on a number of particulars,

most importantly in the chronological presentation of events. Tāranātha places the incident of "Mañjushrī's sword," and recognition of Shāntideva as an accomplished master, *before* his entry into monastic life at Nālandā. Butön does the reverse. Pezzali opts for the order given by Tāranātha, considering it incomprehensible that Shāntideva should have become a royal bodyguard after being a monk at Nālandā. In so doing, she is perhaps betraying a Western prejudice, assuming, possibly on the basis of Christian precedents, that it would be normal for monastic renunciation to come at the end of a worldly career. But from the point of view of Indian Buddhism, and also Tibetan Buddhism (where the same tendency is observable to this day), the order of events given by Butön, and followed by Kunzang Palden, is more plausible, namely a moment of renunciation followed by a period of training in the monastery (admittedly of an extraordinary kind), culminating in the abandonment of clerical restrictions and the embracing of the lifestyle of a wandering siddha. Indeed, the story of Busukhuwa, in the lives of the eighty-four mahāsiddhas, seems clearly to refer to Shāntideva; and the tantric aspect of the lives of the mahāsiddhas will perhaps explain the presence in the Tibetan Tengyur of tantric commentaries attributed to Shāntideva.

117. Shāstra (Tib. bstan bcos)—a commentary specifically illustrating the meaning of the Buddha's words. The three qualifications for composing shāstras are perfect spiritual realization, the vision of the yidam deity, and a complete knowledge of the five sciences.

118. Now in modern Gujarat.

119. Tib. 'jam dpal rnon po'i sgrub thabs, a sādhana, or meditative practice, based on the bodhisattva Mañjushrī, performed with a view to the development of intelligence and sharp faculties. The fact that Shāntideva had a vision of Mañjushrī means that he became fully accomplished in the sādhana.

120. According to tradition, still observed today, Shāntideva assumed an element of the name of his ordaining abbot.

121. See note 130.

122. I.e., study, meditation, and religious exercises such as prostration and circumambulation.

123. I.e., a throne supported by eight carved lions. The lion throne is traditionally the seat for the teaching of the Dharma. The Buddha is nearly always depicted as seated upon a lion throne. The intention of the monks is obviously ironical and insulting.

124. See chap. 5, verses 105–106.

125. Tib. *mchod rten dpal yon can.*

126. The name of a Hindu deity. A maṇḍala is a design, usually two-dimensional, representing the celestial abode of a deity and much used in tantric ritual and meditation.

127. See B. Bhattacharya, *Foreword to the Tattvasamgraha* (Baroda, 1926). Here Bhattacharya announces his discovery of the *Tattvasiddhi*, a hitherto unknown tantric treatise in Sanskrit. The colophon declares and, according to Bhattacharya, the style of the document confirms, that the text was composed by Shāntarakṣhita.

128. Perhaps an emblematic figure. Eleven of these commentaries were translated into Tibetan. See Bibliography.

129. Kawa Peltsek (ka ba dpal brtsegs)—one of the earliest and greatest of all Tibetan translators and a disciple of Guru Padmasambhava. Although not one of the "seven who were tried," i.e., the first seven Tibetans to embrace the monastic life (so called because their ordination was an experiment commanded by King Trisong Detsen in the year 767, to establish whether Tibetans were capable of monastic commitment), Kawa Peltsek was nevertheless ordained shortly afterwards, and no doubt by Shāntarakṣhita.

130. The *Shikṣhāsamuchchaya* still exists in Sanskrit, and a Tibetan translation (Tib. *bslab btus*) is preserved in the Tengyur. The *Sūtrasamuchchaya* (Tib. *mdo btus*) has been lost. Indeed, the existence of a *Sūtrasamuchchaya* by Shāntideva, distinct from the work of the same name attributed to Nāgārjuna, has been questioned by Western scholarship. See Pezzali, op. cit.

131. Great "selfhood": i.e., the state in which the duality of self and other is totally transcended.

132. It is recorded that once, when Maitriyogin was teaching, someone threw a stone at a barking dog so that the animal was badly injured. Maitriyogin gave a scream of pain and fell from the throne on which he was sitting. To the astonishment and embarrassment of the disciples, who had been inclined to dismiss the master's behavior as an exaggerated theatrical performance, Maitriyogin pulled up his shirt so that they could see a great wound on his side, in exactly the same place where the dog had been struck.

133. It is recorded in the *Mahābhiniṣhkramana* that Devadatta, the cousin of Prince Siddhārtha, took a bow and arrow and shot down a swan. The creature was grounded but not killed. The future Buddha took the bird

upon his knees and comforted it. Devadatta sent to claim his prize, no doubt intending to kill it, but the Buddha refused to hand over the swan, saying that the bird was his. An exquisite description of the incident is to be found in *The Light of Asia* by Sir Edwin Arnold:

> . . . Then our Lord
> Laid the swan's neck beside his own smooth cheek
> And gravely spake, "Say no! the bird is mine,
> The first of myriad things that shall be mine
> By right of mercy and love's lordliness. . . .

134. This is a reference to Machig Labdrön, the great Tibetan yoginī and disciple of the Indian master Padampa Sangye. She is particularly celebrated as the propagator of *chöd (gcod)*, a meditative practice in which an offering is made of one's own body as sustenance for malevolent spirits.

135. This means that, excluding mere randomness, they cannot be shown to be directly produced by their antecedents. In other words, it is impossible to express in conceptual terms the relationship, causal or otherwise, linking the two terms.

136. This verse is taken from the *Fundamental Treatise on the Middle Way (Mūlamādhyamikakārikā)* by Nāgārjuna.

137. That is, between the antecedent and the consequent.

138. This means that when a moment of consciousness passes, a new one arises identical to it in nature—i.e., mere cognizance—but varying in "color" according to karmic circumstances. The point being made is that there is simply a continuum of interlinked moments, but there is no *substratum*, no underlying entity, that endures as the "experiencer" of a stream of extrinsic events.

BIBLIOGRAPHY

The following are the names of the Sanskrit commentaries on the *Bodhicharyāvatāra* (of which, however, only eight are complete) translated and preserved in the Tibetan Tengyur. Only one full commentary (by Prajñākaramati) and fragments of a few others have survived in Sanskrit (see Pezzali, p. 47). In the references, *P.* refers to the Tibetan Tripiṭaka Peking edition (see Tokyo-Kyoto: Susuki Research Foundation, 1956, which is a reprint of this); *C.* refers to *Catalogue of Kanjur and Tanjur* by Alaka Chattopadhyaya (Calcutta: Indo-Tibetan Studies, 1972); and *T.* refers to *Guide to the Nyingma Edition of the* sDe-dge bKa'-'gyur/bsTan-'gyur by Tarthang Tulku (Berkeley: Dharma Publishing, 1980).

Byang chub kyi spyod pa la 'jug pa'i dka' 'grel (Bodhicharyāvatāra-pañjikā). Prajñākaramati (Shesrab 'byung gnas blo gros). P. 5273, vol. 100. T. 3872.

Byang chub sems dpa'i spyod pa la 'jug pa'i rnam par bshad pa'i bka' 'grel (Bodhisattvacharyāvatāra-vivriti-pañjikā), in 9 chapters. Krishnapa. P. 5274, vol. 100. T. 3873.

Byang chub sems dpa'i spyod pa la 'jug pa'i legs par sbyar ba (Bodhisattvacharyāvatāra-saṃskāra), in 10 chapters. Kalyāṇadeva. P. 5275, vol. 100. T. 3874.

*Byang chub sems dpa'i spyod pa la 'jug pa'i rtogs par dka' ba'i gnas gtan la dbab pa zhes bya ba'i gzhung (Bodhisattvacharyāvatāra-duravabodha[pāda]nirṇayanāma-grantha).*Krishṇapāda, alias Kālapa/Nagphowa. P. 5276, vol. 100. T. 3875.

Byang chub sems dpa'i spyod pa la 'jug pa'i dka' 'grel (Bodhisattvacharyāvatārapañjikā). Vairochanarakshita of Vikramashīla. P. 5277, vol. 100. T. 3875A.

Shes rab le'u'i dka' 'grel (Prajñāpariccheda-pañjikā), commentary on the ninth chapter. Author unknown. P. 5278, vol. 100. T. 3876.

Byang chub sems dpa'i spyod pa la 'jug pa'i rnam par bshad pa (Bodhisattva-charyāvatāravivṛiti), commentary on chapters 9 and 10. Author unknown, possibly Dānashīla. P. 5279, vol. 100.

Bodhisattvacharyāvatāra-prajñāparicccheda-pariṇamana-pañjikā (byang chub sems dpa'i spyod pa la 'jug pa'i shes rab le'u dang bsngo ba'i dka' 'grel. Author unknown. T. 3877.

Byang chub sems dpa'i spyod pa la 'jug pa'i don sum cu rtsa drug bsdus pa (Bodhi-sattvacharyāvatāra-ṣhaṭṭriṃshat-piṇḍārtha). Dharmapāla (gser gling bla ma chos skyong). P. 5280, vol. 100. T. 3878.

Byang chub sems dpa'i spyod pa la 'jug pa'i don bsdus pa (Bodhisattvacharyāva-tāra-piṇḍārtha). Dharmapāla (gser gling bla ma chos skyong). P. 5281, vol. 100. T. 3879.

Byang chub kyi spyod pa la 'jug pa'i dgongs pa'i 'grel pa khyad par gsal byed ces bya ba (Bodhicharyāvatāra-tātparya-pañjikā-visheṣhadyotanī-nāma), commentary on all 10 chapters. Vibhūtichandra. P. 5282, vol. 100. T. 3880.

Byang chub sems dpa'i spyod pa la 'jug pa'i mdo cam gdams ngag tu byas pa (Bodhisattvacharyā-sūtrīkṛitāvāda). Dīpamkarajñāna (dpal mar me mjad ye shes). P. 5348, vol. 103.

Bodhisattvacharyāvatāra-bhāṣhya. Dīpaṃkarashrījñāna. C. mdo xxvii 5.210a: 5–223b:2.

Byang chub sems dpa' spyod pa bsdus pa'i sgron ma rin po che'i phreng ba. (Bodhisattvacharyā-[saṃgraha]-pradīpa-ratnamālā). Dhārmika-subhūtighoṣha. mdo xxx 31.389b:1–395a:4. T. 3936.

✿ WORKS CITED

Arnold, Sir Edwin. *The Light of Asia*. Reprint. London: Routledge and Kegan Paul, 1978.

Batchelor, Stephen, trans. *A Guide to the Bodhisattva's Way of Life*. A translation from the Tibetan of the *Bodhicharyāvatāra* of Shāntideva. Dharamsala: Library of Tibetan Works and Archives, 1979.

Barnett, L. D., trans. *The Path of Light*. Abridged translation from the Sanskrit of the *Bodhicaryāvatāra*. London: Wisdom of the East, 1909.

Crosby, Kate, and Andrew Skilton, trans. *The Bodhicharyāvatāra*. Translated from the Sanskrit. Oxford: Oxford University Press, 1996.

Dalai Lama, H.H. *A Flash of Lightning in the Dark of Night: A Guide to the Bodhisattva's Way of Life*. A commentary on the ninth chapter of the *Bodhicharyāvatāra*. Boston & London: Shambhala Publications, 1994.

———. *Path to Bliss: A Practical Guide to Stages of Meditation*. Translated by Geshe Thubten Jinpa. Edited by Christine Cox. Ithaca, N.Y.: Snow Lion Publications, 1991.

———. *Transcendent Wisdom: A Commentary on the Ninth Chapter of Shāntideva's Guide to the Bodhisattva Way of Life*. Translated, edited and annotated by B. Alan Wallace. Ithaca, N.Y.: Snow Lion Publications, 1988.

Dilgo Khyentse Rinpoche. *The Heart Treasure of the Enlightened Ones*. Boston & London: Shambhala Publications, 1992.

Dowman, Keith. *Masters of Mahāmudrā: Songs and Histories of the Eighty-Four Buddhist Siddhas*. Albany: State University of New York Press, 1985.

Driessens, Georges, trans. *Traité du Milieu*, translation from the Tibetan of *Mūlamādhyamikakārikā of Nāgārjuna*. Paris: Editions du Seuil, 1995.

Driessens, Georges, trans. *Vivre en héros pour l'éveil*, translation from the Tibetan of *Bodhicharyāvatāra* of Shāntideva. Paris: Editions du Seuil, 1993.

Finot, Louis, trans. *La Marche à la lumière*, translation from the Sanskrit of the *Bodhicharyāvatāra*. Paris: Ed. Bossard, 1920. Paris: Ed. Les Deux Océans, 1987.

Gendun Chöpel. *To Follow the Virtuous Life*, translation from the Tibetan of the *Bodhicharyāvatāra*, original manuscript in the Library of Tibetan Works and Archives, Dharamsala, India.

Hiriyanna, M. *The Essentials of Indian Philosophy*. Delhi: Motilal Banarsidass, 1995.

Kelsang Gyatso, Geshe. *Meaningful to Behold: An Oral Commentary to Shāntideva's A Guide to the Bodhisattva's Way of Life*. Cumbria, England: Wisdom Publications, 1980.

Kunzang Palden. Commentary on *Bodhicharyāvatāra: Byang chub sems dpa'i spyod pa la 'jug pa'i tsig 'grel 'jam dbyang bla ma'i zhal lung bdud rtsi'i thig pa*. Text established by Zenkar Rinpoche, Thubten Nyima, of the Sichuan People's Publishing House, Chengtu, China; also vol. 1 of *Collected works of mkhan-po kun-bzang dpal-ldan*, published by Lama Ngödrup for Kyabje Dilgo Khyentse Rinpoche, Paro, Bhutan, 1982.

———. *Wisdom: Two Buddhist Commentaries*, book one: *The Nectar of Mañjushrī's Speech*, commentary on *Bodhicharyāvatāra*, chapter 9. Saint Léon-sur-Vézère: Editions Padmakara, 1993.

La marche vers l'éveil. Translation of *Bodhicharyāvatāra* by Louis Finot, re-edited with corrections. Saint Léon-sur-Vézère: Editions Padmakara, 1992.

Matics, Marion L., trans. *Entering the Path of Enlightenment*, translation from the Sanskrit of *Bodhicharyāvatāra*. New York: Macmillan, 1970.

Minyak Kunzang Sönam. *Commentary on the Wisdom Chapter of the Bodhicharyāvatāra: spyod 'jug shes rab le'u gzhung 'grel zab mo rten 'byung gi de kho na nyid yang gsel sgron me.* Great Printing Press of Derge, Tibet, and Bod kyi shes rigs dpar khang, Beijing, 1990.

———. *Wisdom: Two Buddhist Commentaries*, book two: *The Brilliant Torch*, commentary on *Bodhicharyāvatāra*, chapter 9. Saint Léon-sur-Vézère: Editions Padmakara, 1993.

Murti, T.R.V. *The Central Philosophy of Buddhism*. London: George Allen and Unwin, 1955.

Pezzali, Amalia. *Śāntideva, mystique bouddhiste des VIIe et VIIIe siècles*. Florence: Vallecchi Editore, 1968.

Sangharakshita, Bhikshu. *A Survey of Buddhism*. Bangalore: The Indian Institute of World Culture, 1957; new edition by Windhorse Publications.

Shāntideva. Tibetan translation of *Bodhicharyāvatāra: byang chub sems dpa'i spyod pa la 'jug pa.* Text established by Zenkar Rinpoche, Thubten Nyima, of the Sichuan People's Publishing House, Chengtu, China.

Tāranātha. *History of Buddhism in India (rgya gar 'phags pa'i yul gyi chos 'byung)*, Thimpu, Bhutan: Kunzang Topgay, 1976. English translation: *Tāranātha's History of Buddhism in India*. Translated by Lama Chimpa and Alaka Chattopadhyaya. Atlantic Highlands, N.J.: Humanities Press, 1970.

Yeshe Peljor. *dpag bsam ljon bzang*, trans. and ed. by Shri Sarat Chandra Das with the title *The History of the Rise, Progress and Downfall of Buddhism in India*, Calcutta, 1908.

(Continued on next page)

The Way of a Pilgrim and The Pilgrim Continues His Way. Translated by Olga Savin.

When Things Fall Apart: Heart Advice for Difficult Times, by Pema Chödrön.

The Wisdom of No Escape and the Path of Loving-Kindness, by Pema Chödrön.

The Wisdom of the Prophet: Sayings of Muhammad. Translated by Thomas Cleary.

The Yoga-Sūtra of Patañjali: A New Translation with Commentary. Translated by Chip Hartranft.